Ian Black is Vicar of Whitkirk, Leeds. H
in Kent and has been involved in post-o
dioceses of Canterbury and Ripon & Le
Canterbury Cathedral and has been a prison chaplain. Ian trained at
Lincoln Theological College and prior to ordination was a tax
accountant. He is married with two sons.

INTERCESSIONS

for the Calendar of Saints and Holy Days

IAN BLACK

First published in Great Britain in 2005

Society for Promoting Christian Knowledge
36 Causton Street
London SW1P 4ST

British Library Cataloguing-in-Publication Data
A catalogue record for this book is available from the British Library

ISBN 0–281–05747–8

10 9 8 7 6 5 4 3 2 1

Typeset by Graphicraft Ltd., Hong Kong
Printed in Great Britain by Ashford Colour Press

Contents

———◆◆◆———

In Part One, entries in capitals indicate Principal Feasts, those in regular type indicate Festivals, and those in italic indicate Lesser Festivals.

---

* This intercession can also be used for other festivals of the Blessed Virgin Mary: the Blessed Virgin Mary (15 August); the Birth of the Blessed Virgin Mary (8 September); and the Conception of the Blessed Virgin Mary (8 December).

Contents

Contents

To Peter and John,
Susan, James and Michael,
and all whose sharing of themselves
has been an inspiration for these prayers.

Introduction

————◦◦◦————

The inspiration for writing this collection of intercessions was born
through a growing and deepening appreciation of the Calendar of
Saints and Holy Days. In keeping these days I have come to value
them enormously. They provide worked examples of living holiness in
practice. The individuals concerned are a varied lot, to say the least, and
there are no plaster cast statues here. Engaging with their stories moves
our spirituality from a mere cosy feeling to connect with the bite and
grit of life. It is because these people's Christian faith was grounded in
the bite and grit of living that when we stand in their presence we are
on holy ground. There is no escapism here; rather we are drawn deeper
into the struggles and hopes of real Christian living.

When we add to this the major festivals, we are encouraged to engage
with the heart of our faith. It takes us away from the churchy concerns
that can so weigh us down to concentrate on the faith that fires us and
in turn draws us towards the gathering together that becomes the
Church. Further reference can be made to works like *Exciting Holiness*,
which gives biographical information for the people commemorated in
the Calendar together with the appropriate readings set for their day.
This collection forms a natural companion to that compendium. (See
Suggested Further Resources on page 140.)

The other side of these prayers coming to birth lies, paradoxically, in
some spiritually arid moments; the occasions when I have stood at the
altar presiding at the Eucharist, invited the congregation to join in prayer
for the Church and the world . . . and then found myself completely dry
or just too tired to come up with anything. On these occasions I would
have welcomed some prayers to fall back on and hold me, even rescue
me. If that is your experience, either when preparing intercessions for
the next day or literally at the moment of leading intercessions, then feel
free to borrow these.

These intercessions are a response of prayer to the stories, events and concepts of faith that we celebrate in the Church of England Calendar. They can be used straight, adapted to suit particular places or occasions, or just as a prompt to get you started with preparing your own. They are for clergy and lay people: anyone who leads intercessions in whatever setting. They can be used corporately or in private as an aid to personal devotion.

They have been written in an Anglican context. They therefore include prayers for our bishop. To Anglicans the bishop has a special place in the life of the Church and as the focus for the Church's unity. Prayer for the bishop is also prayer for the wider Church and our place in it. In other church contexts these can be adapted with minimum effort.

Each set of intercessions has been given its own bidding and congregational response to intersperse the sections. These are optional, and in some settings familiar forms from the regular liturgy may be more appropriate. Alternatively the bidding provided here can be combined with a more customary response. The time of prayer can also be begun and ended in whatever form custom or occasion requires. The final petition is designed to end with a clear and corporate 'Amen', or to act as an introduction to the Common Worship (or other) conclusion. With slight adaptation, it could lead into the Lord's Prayer.

There are also points where the intercessions encourage the addition of either names or particular intentions from the locality. These are indicated by [. . .]. This is usually in the prayer for the Church, where a cycle of prayer could be used; and also in the prayers for the sick and departed, where certain traditions would naturally include specific names.

The intercessions are grouped in two parts.

Part One covers the Principal Feasts and Festivals from the Calendar. Chapter 1 follows a chronological calendar of the days and Chapter 2 picks up the dates that vary according to the liturgical year (e.g. Easter and Pentecost). Also included are a number of Lesser Festivals that stand alone and are not caught by the general Lesser Festivals and Commemorations of Part Two (e.g. Anne and Joachim, 26 July; Remembrance, 11 November; and All Souls, 2 November). Provision is included for the patron saints of the UK, even though two are Lesser Festivals and could be covered by the general prayers; and also for Valentine as a response to the secular tone of his day.

Part Two contains general prayers following the designations that are ascribed to each of the Lesser Festivals and Commemorations. So, where someone is remembered as a 'Bishop' or 'Social Reformer', there is a set of generally focused prayers for use on that day. In three instances I have further sub-divided the designations for clarity: 'Bishops' and 'Pastors'; 'Spiritual Writers and Mystics' and 'Teachers of the Faith'; 'Social Reformers' and 'Those Working with the Poor and Underprivileged'.

Finally there are two additional sets which will be of significance for many: Harvest and Memorial. Harvest is a festival that most churches keep. It doesn't fall on a particular day, just some time in September or October. Provision is included here because harvest is one of those days when resources are always needed; it is a 'popular holy day', though not strictly found in the Calendar. Many churches now have regular memorial or bereavement services where those connected with a funeral in the preceding period are invited to a special service. Although there are similarities with All Souls' Day, there is also a sufficiently distinctive flavour to these services to warrant a separate set of prayers.

These intercessions have been road-tested in real churches. I am grateful to the people of those places who have provided the test track for them and whose communal and pastoral life has fed into them. I hope they will assist with a prayerful encounter with God, who is the source of all holiness.

Ian Black

Part One

PRINCIPAL FEASTS, FESTIVALS AND SELECTED LESSER FESTIVALS

1

A Calendar of Feasts and Festivals

THE NAMING AND CIRCUMCISION OF JESUS

Festival

1 January

Jesus, name above all names
Incline your ear to our prayer.

Jesus, Saviour,
at your name every knee should bow
and every tongue confess that you are Lord.
At the beginning of a new year we dedicate afresh our lives
   in your service.
We place before you our hopes and dreams,
our regrets and resolutions.
Keep us faithful to the covenant of your grace.

Jesus, name above all names
Incline your ear to our prayer.

Jesus, through your victory on the cross we are adopted
   as heirs of your glory.
We pray for the Church, for *N* our bishop and all who rejoice
   in your name . . .
Refresh all who are baptized in your name to proclaim your love and
   announce your salvation.

Jesus, name above all names
Incline your ear to our prayer.

Jesus, as you were circumcised into the covenant with Abraham,
we pray for all who share a spiritual ancestry with Abraham and Sarah.
Unite the peoples of the earth in a common humanity
and keep before us the path of justice and peace.
We pray for all governments and rulers.

Jesus, name above all names
Incline your ear to our prayer.

Jesus, redeemer and Lord of all,
we pray for all who suffer in any way . . .
We pray for children struggling for breath in the first days of their lives;
for all who are anxious and fearful.
Give us confidence to trust in you and your bountiful providence.

Jesus, name above all names
Incline your ear to our prayer.

Jesus, whose blood was shed
in circumcision in accordance with the Law
and on the cross for our redemption,
we pray for all who have died . . .
Bring us at the last to rise with you in glory.

Jesus, name above all names
Incline your ear to our prayer.

As we celebrate your new creation, where saints are made perfect, we
commend ourselves and all for whom we pray to your saving love.

THE EPIPHANY OF OUR LORD

Principal Feast

6 January

God of wonder and of joy
Lead us by the light of your presence.

Lord, we kneel in adoration before the throne of your grace among us
    in your Son.
As a pilgrim people drawn to worship,
move us in our faith by your leading Spirit,
that we may recognize you in unexpected places and people.
We offer you the incense of our praise and honour the holiness
    of your name.
Bless all who lead worship, that your presence may be made known.
Inspire our vision and give us thankful hearts for your generous
    goodness.

God of wonder and of joy
Lead us by the light of your presence.

Lord, we come laden with treasures and desires
and lay them all before your transforming love.
We offer you our gold, our money, our power and choices.
Preserve us from turning these into our god
and seeking to subvert your will in our trading and labour.
We place before your Son all that we are and all that we have.
Make us wise stewards of your bounty.

God of wonder and of joy
Lead us by the light of your presence.

Lord, we come in search of wholeness and healing,
bringing spices to anoint, to fragrance, to heal.
We pray for all who work to heal the mind, the body and the spirit;
for those who give dignity to the dying

5

and all going through a vale of pain or misery . . .
In all times, in all seasons,
give us grace to proclaim your saving and reconciling love.

God of wonder and of joy
Lead us by the light of your presence.

We lay before you all who have died and behold your glory . . .
Comfort all who carry the pain and loss of grief deep within them.
Shine into our hearts the light of your redeeming love.

God of wonder and of joy
Lead us by the light of your presence.

As we worship and adore the light of your glory made known in your
Son, so we place all our prayers before your eternal love.

THE CONVERSION OF PAUL, APOSTLE

Festival

25 January

God of our transformation
Fill us with your grace.

Lord of light and power,
we celebrate the dramatic conversion of Saul
from breathing threats and murder against your Church
to become Paul the apostle of your Son.
We give thanks for the leadership he gave to the fledgling Church;
for his letters which continue to inspire and nurture faith today.
We pray for all whose lives
have been touched by a profound experience of your loving presence
    and call.
Fire us with a passion to tell of your wonderful deeds.

God of our transformation
Fill us with your grace.

As we come to the end of the Week of Prayer for Christian Unity
we pray for all Christians,
for a strengthening of the bonds that unite
and a deeper commitment to work through our differences, however
    strongly held.
We pray for *N* our bishop and all who focus the unity of the
    Church . . .
Draw all labourers of your harvest into a closer fellowship of your name.

God of our transformation
Fill us with your grace.

Ananias and the saints of Damascus were startled at the sudden change of
    Paul's heart.
Keep us open to your transforming power,

7

to believe change is possible in others and ourselves.
We pray for those having difficulty convincing others that their new life
   is genuine
and those whose pain makes them suspicious.

God of our transformation
Fill us with your grace.

Saul was sent on a journey fired by hatred and fear,
but found himself embarking on a mission set ablaze with faith, hope
   and love.
We pray for all policy-makers and those who send envoys to do their
   bidding.
Give us all humility to question the motives that drive us
and grace to work for the good of all.

God of our transformation
Fill us with your grace.

Paul spent time recovering and reassessing his life.
We pray for all who offer hospitality for recuperation
   and refocusing of vision.
We pray for all in need of convalescence and healing . . .
Fill them with your Holy Spirit and strengthen us all for your praise
   and service.

God of our transformation
Fill us with your grace.

God of glory, we hold in your presence those who have died . . .
Comfort all who grieve.
Fill us all with the hope of Christ raised from the dead.

God of our transformation
Fill us with your grace.

Rejoicing with Paul, Ananias and all who have believed that there
would be a fulfilment of your word, we entrust all our prayers to your
transforming love.

CANDLEMAS
THE PRESENTATION OF CHRIST IN
THE TEMPLE

Principal Feast

2 February

Lord, we praise your name
Your word has been fulfilled.

We celebrate today Christ being presented in the temple,
acclaimed as the glory of Israel and a light to lighten all peoples.
We pray for the Church, that it may share his light and reflect his glory.
We pray for *N* our bishop,
this parish/church and all with whom we share the name of Christ . . .
We give thanks for all who have carried the torch of faith in the past,
all who have tended the light and helped it shine from this place,
who have sat in the temple and longed to see the fulfilment of promise.
May we in our generation be faithful witnesses to your saving love.

Lord, we praise your name
Your word has been fulfilled.

Faithful Simeon spoke of your Son exposing the inner thoughts of many,
of him being a sign that will be opposed.
We pray for all who have positions of responsibility, all whose decisions
    affect others.
We pray for all who sit in our Parliament, all who represent us
    internationally;
for peace with justice, for honesty and integrity.
We pray for all involved in broadcast and print media;
for those who seek to call leaders to account;
for honest and just reporting.

Lord, we praise your name
Your word has been fulfilled.

As we hear of the offering made for your Son being the poor person's
  offering,
we pray for all who struggle on low incomes,
all who are hungry,
all refugees from political and natural disasters.
Give us generous hearts to show your light in ways that bless and heal.
We give thanks for all who take an interest in children and who inspire
  the young.
We pray for good role models and for people of good will
to nurture and guide those seeking direction in their lives.

Lord, we praise your name
Your word has been fulfilled.

We pray for all whose hope has been damaged,
whose hearts have grown cold and whose expectation has turned to
  cynicism.
We pray for any struggling with infirmity or any kind of illness . . .
Lord, we look for redemption and seek your healing power.

Lord, we praise your name
Your word has been fulfilled.

Heavenly Father, we pray for all who, like Mary, know the pain of their
  hearts being pierced;
for grieving parents,
all who have lost loved ones and who feel a deep sorrow within
  them . . .
We pray for all faithful servants departed and who now see your
  salvation.

Lord, we praise your name
Your word has been fulfilled.

As faithful Simeon and Anna praised you for the holy child, may our
hearts resound with songs of thankfulness and praise. May we sing of
your glory in ways of holiness and righteousness all the days of our life.

VALENTINE, MARTYR, *c.* AD 269

Commemoration

14 February

God of love
You bring us to delight in your goodness.

All-loving God, you show your love in your Son Jesus Christ.
Through his life and passion,
his death and resurrection,
you reveal the all-consuming heights that love can reach.
Fill our hearts with this passionate embrace, that it may overflow to all
   we meet.

God of love
You bring us to delight in your goodness.

As we commemorate Valentine,
his selfless martyrdom for your glory,
we pray for all whose loving brings them into conflict with hatred and
   violence.
We pray for all who suffer for their faith,
those well known
and those about whom we know nothing at all, but you know them
   nonetheless.
We pray for the Church inspired by the blood of martyrs,
for *N* our bishop and all with the courage to speak of your love
   and glory . . .

God of love
You bring us to delight in your goodness.

We give thanks for those whom we love,
those who love us and who teach us how to love.
We pray for all who are married,
all who have committed themselves to a covenant in your grace,

those preparing for marriage
and any whose relationships are encountering difficulties or have recently
    fractured.
We pray for the work of Relate and all relationship counsellors.

God of love
You bring us to delight in your goodness.

In a world that can seem so full of hatred and strife,
we pray for those who hold the cords of power
and those with vision to turn love into policies
    for the mutual benefit of all.
We pray for all whose work places their relationships under strain
or leaves little space for them.

God of love
You bring us to delight in your goodness.

We pray for all living out vows promised
in sickness and in health,
for better and for worse.
We hold before you all who are ill
or for whom we are aware of a special need . . .
We pray for those for whom caring is a duty of love and those finding it
    hard to bear;
for any who have seen the one they love diminished by a debilitating
    condition.
Enfold them in your loving arms and bring them the comfort of your
    healing Spirit.

God of love
You bring us to delight in your goodness.

Lord, whose love is strong as death, you love everything you have made.
Be with all who mourn and whose hearts are heavy with grief.
We pray for the inconsolable,
those at a loss to know where to turn,
as well as those thankful for lives shared.
We pray for the departed, especially any we have known and loved . . .
With you is life everlasting.

God of love
You bring us to delight in your goodness.

Rejoicing in communion with Valentine and men and women of holiness throughout the ages, we commit all our prayers to your loving mercy.

DAVID, PATRON SAINT OF WALES, *c.* AD 601

Lesser Festival

1 March

Bountiful Lord
We bless your name.

God of oceans, wind and fire,
mountain range and valley floor,
hear the prayer we bring before your face.
Thank you for inspiring your servant David to found
    monasteries of prayer
and to keep vigil through the silent hours.
Teach us to honour his example of simplicity
that we may celebrate your providential care all the more.

Bountiful Lord
We bless your name.

Lord, you feed us with the bread of life
and nurture us with spiritual milk.
We pray for the Church's mission;
for the Church in Wales and in this place.
We pray for *N* our bishop and all spiritual leaders . . .
Inspire our faith and fill us with a profound hope in your Son Jesus Christ.

Bountiful Lord
We bless your name.

God our stronghold and sure defence,
we pray for all to whom we entrust government;
for the Welsh Assembly and all regional tiers of government.
Refresh and renew our political life.
Keep apathy and cynicism from our doors.
We hold before you all who benefit from provision
    out of our common purse.

We pray for places of industry and commerce;
for regeneration programmes
and those being retrained for new work
or in long-established sources of employment.

Bountiful Lord
We bless your name.

Compassionate God,
we make special intention for the sick and infirm;
for all who hunger and thirst;
for those suffering from addictions and dependencies,
and for treatment programmes . . .

Bountiful Lord
We bless your name.

Living Lord, we lay before you all who have died . . .
Look with compassion on all who mourn.
Bring us at the last to share with all your saints in glory everlasting.

Bountiful Lord
We bless your name.

In communion with David and all the saints of the British Isles, we
commend all people to your saving love.

PATRICK, PATRON SAINT OF IRELAND,
c. AD **460**

Lesser Festival

17 March

Our pride is in the name of the Lord
Answer us when we call.

God of the free and of all enslaved,
we bind ourselves to the name of your Trinity.
We thank you for calling your servant Patrick to trust in you in strength
   and danger,
to proclaim your love to the people of Ireland.
Surround us with the breastplate of your presence.
Give us the same trust and fortitude,
whatever opposition or ridicule we may face.

Our pride is in the name of the Lord
Answer us when we call.

Ever present Christ,
be with your Church here and everywhere.
Bless the Church in Ireland.
Deepen the bonds of understanding and respect between the different
   traditions,
that those who call themselves after your name
may model for others the path of peace and good will to all people.
We pray for *N* our bishop and all Christians, especially those
   we disagree with . . .
May our allegiance be to you before all else.

Our pride is in the name of the Lord
Answer us when we call.

High King of heaven, Lord of lords,
the one to whom we owe true allegiance,

we pray for those who exercise authority for the good of all.
Open before us the way of justice.
Give them wisdom to use the power they have with courage and
    fairness,
showing partiality to no one.

Our pride is in the name of the Lord
Answer us when we call.

Watch, dear Lord, with those whose strength is weakened
by illness or increased infirmity.
We pray for all undergoing tests for what is at present unknown,
those struck by tragedy,
and whose hearts are breaking as they watch by the side of someone
    they love . . .
We place them in the circle of your love and healing presence.

Our pride is in the name of the Lord
Answer us when we call.

Christ who came for love of our love,
who died that we might live
and who has opened to us the gates of heaven,
hear us as we remember in prayer all who have died . . .
Restore us in your image,
comfort us in our grief
and bring your salvation to the ends of the earth.

Our pride is in the name of the Lord
Answer us when we call.

Holy Trinity, Father, Son and Holy Spirit, by the invocation of your
name we offer these prayers in faith.

JOSEPH OF NAZARETH

Festival

19 March

Father God
Fulfil your promise to your servants.

Heavenly Father,
you entrusted your Son to the care and guardianship of Joseph.
Through him he was adopted into the royal line of David
so that the hopes and longings of your people may be fulfilled.
We thank you that we are adopted through grace as your children.
Anoint us with the seal of your Spirit, that the world may resound with
    your praise.

Father God
Fulfil your promise to your servants.

As Joseph trusted in you,
despite his inclination quietly to put Mary away,
we pray for the Church,
that it may be a place where faith can be energized and strengthened for
    your service,
a place prepared to risk what others may see as scandalous
for the sake of your good news.
We pray for *N* our bishop
and all who embrace the prompting of your Spirit
    with courage and hope . . .

Father God
Fulfil your promise to your servants.

Warned in a dream,
Joseph took your Holy Child and his mother to safety in Egypt.
We pray for those who have to act to protect the young;
for child protection advisers, social workers
and those who do not turn a blind eye to abuse and neglect.

We pray for all who take care of children as their own;
for step-parents, foster parents, those who adopt and legal guardians.
We pray for politicians and policy-makers,
for all who are charged with ensuring the vulnerable are protected.

Father God
Fulfil your promise to your servants.

As Joseph followed a trade as a carpenter,
we lay before you our work and creating.
Expand our understanding of ministry and vocation
to embrace how we earn our living.
Teach us to make drudgery divine
and to encounter you through all we do with our hands.
May your transforming presence challenge and redeem even the most
  mundane tasks.

Father God
Fulfil your promise to your servants.

Joseph disappears from the story some time after your Son was 12 years
  old.
We pray for widows who bring up children as single parents,
for children whose fathers die while they are young.
We pray for all in any kind of need . . .
Lord, your grace is always sufficient for all we have to face.
Hold those for whom we pray in your loving care.

Father God
Fulfil your promise to your servants.

We give thanks for those who have shown a father's love to us,
for those who have guided and nurtured us as we have grown.
We remember before you all who have died . . .
Turn the darkness of death into the light and peace of your salvation.

Father God
Fulfil your promise to your servants.

God of our ancestors, as we rejoice with Joseph and Blessed Mary, we
entrust our prayers to your gracious mercy.

THE ANNUNCIATION OF OUR LORD TO THE BLESSED VIRGIN MARY

Principal Feast

25 March

This intercession can also be used for other festivals of the Blessed Virgin Mary:

The Blessed Virgin Mary (Festival, 15 August)
The Birth of the Blessed Virgin Mary (Lesser Festival/Festival, 8 September)
The Conception of the Blessed Virgin Mary (Lesser Festival, 8 December)

God of our salvation
Let it be according to your word.

Holy God, you bring the mystery of your love to flower in the consent
of Blessed Mary.
As she bore your eternal Word made flesh,
so may he always find a welcome in our hearts,
that our lives may magnify you and we may rejoice in your salvation.
We pray for the Church, that it may be a faithful midwife for the
gospel;
for *N* our bishop and all with whom we share the name of Christ . . .
Give to us the same obedience to your will,
that with courage and thankfulness we may echo Mary's prayer:
'Behold, the servant of the Lord'.

God of our salvation
Let it be according to your word.

Sovereign Lord, you alone rule in our hearts and we delight in your
service.
Hear us as we pray for the mighty,
all to whom we give the responsibility of government, and the barons of
industry.
May all who occupy positions of power
avoid the arrogance that seeks to overthrow or subvert your will.

We pray for the lowly,
all who are affected by the policies of others
and have little influence on the direction of that policy.

God of our salvation
Let it be according to your word.

God of charity, whose compassion sets our priorities on their heads,
we pray for the hungry and homeless, for day centres and night shelters;
for all who are in debt and at the mercy of unscrupulous moneylenders.
We pray for aid agencies, for fair trade and all involved in co-operatives
    and loan clubs.
We pray for all who are spiritually hungry.
Give us the bread which satisfies, the bread of eternal life.
We hold before you teenage parents
and all wrestling with decisions about whether to continue with
    unplanned pregnancies.

God of our salvation
Let it be according to your word.

Lord, your grace fills us with more than we can desire
and we become expectant with all you promise.
We pray for all new parents, for brothers and sisters getting used to a
    new arrival;
for maternity units and specialist baby units.
May our homes be places of love, security and truth.
We pray for all whose home life is troubled, all whose trust is abused;
for parents under strain, those at breaking point,
all without networks to help or share the pressure.
We pray for the work of Child Line, and all who offer support where it
    is needed.

God of our salvation
Let it be according to your word.

Blessed Lord, you are with us in our joys and sorrows,
hopes and fears,
hear us as we pray for all who are ill;

for children's hospitals and hospices;
for all whose pregnancies are encountering complications.
We hold before you all for whom we have been asked to pray
or carry in our hearts . . .

God of our salvation
Let it be according to your word.

God of purity and love,
you abhor nothing that you have made and restore to your glory all that
   has been lost.
We remember with thanksgiving those who have died . . .
We pray for all who mourn;
for all who, like Mary, know the pain of losing a child.
May we truly know that you are with us.

God of our salvation
Let it be according to your word.

Rejoicing with Blessed Mary and all faithful people, we commit all our
prayers to your gracious mercy.

GEORGE, PATRON SAINT OF ENGLAND,
c. AD **304**

Festival

23 April

The Lord has done great things for us
We will shout for joy.

Faithful God, we thank you for the witness in the face of death of
    George
and all who have endured martyrdom for the sake of the gospel,
those whose deeds are well known and those whose acts are known only
    to you.
We give thanks for all who have made a stand against evil,
whatever form it has taken.
Give us courage to strive valiantly as a disciple of your Son
and to remain faithful all our days.

The Lord has done great things for us
We will shout for joy.

We pray for the Church;
for *N* our bishop and all who carry the torch of faith in our
    generation . . .
We pray for societies and orders that deepen our commitment
and nurture us in our spiritual identity.
Strengthen us with your Holy Spirit
and restore in your Church hope and confidence in your saving love.

The Lord has done great things for us
We will shout for joy.

God of hope and glory, of liberty and unity,
we pray for our country of England and all who share George as their
    patron saint.
We pray for all who take an active interest in our political life.

23

Keep us from the hatred that leads to extremism.
Give us a true patriotism that asks questions and calls those who lead to
account.
We pray for those who serve in the armed forces and those who commit
them to action.
Raise before us the standard of justice and respect for all.

The Lord has done great things for us
We will shout for joy.

We give thanks for all who move our senses through the power of
drama and poetry;
for actors, directors, playwrights and poets.
As we celebrate the rich heritage of prose and insightful drama,
such as we see in William Shakespeare who shares this day,
may its sweet music stir and provoke within us heaven's call.

The Lord has done great things for us
We will shout for joy.

We bring in prayer all who have sowed in tears.
We pray for all who endure persecution for their faith
or for taking a courageous stand against hatred and vice.
We pray for all in special need . . .
Uphold them with your life-restoring and redeeming Spirit.

The Lord has done great things for us
We will shout for joy.

Salvation comes from you alone
and we rejoice in the promise of your resurrection.
We pray for all who have died . . .
Bring us to triumph in the fulfilment of your eternal glory.

The Lord has done great things for us
We will shout for joy.

As we seek the dawning of the new Jerusalem, not only for this land
but for the whole creation, so we commend our prayers to your loving
mercy.

MARK, EVANGELIST

Festival

25 April

Lord, your word is a lantern to our feet
Shine your light upon our path.

Gracious God, we thank you for our inheritance of faith,
for all who have passed on the good news of Jesus Christ through each
    generation.
We give thanks for the Gospels,
for the words of inspiration and revelation open to us through Mark's
    writing.
We pray for those who dedicate themselves to studying the scriptures
and translating them so that they may be accessible to all.
Enlighten our hearts with the good news of your Kingdom.

Lord, your word is a lantern to our feet
Shine your light upon our path.

We pray for the Church,
for all involved in missionary work at home and overseas.
We pray for *N* our bishop . . .
We pray for all who give spiritual counsel and teach us in our faith,
for Sunday school teachers and all who lead activities involving young
    people.
Give to your Church such passion for your gospel
that we may find ways to communicate afresh the saving message
of your self-giving love.

Lord, your word is a lantern to our feet
Shine your light upon our path.

We pray for all who hold political office and direct our common life.
We pray for truth in word, truth in deed.
Empower us and all people of good will with whom we can work

to shape a society where peace and justice are honoured and upheld.
We pray for all who are persecuted for their principles by unjust
  regimes.
May we choose life in all its fullness.

Lord, your word is a lantern to our feet
Shine your light upon our path.

Merciful Lord,
the disciples left everything to follow you.
At the hour of your Son's arrest, some left everything to get away.
Forgive us when we deny your truth,
when we lack courage to stand up for what we believe.
Restore us in your image and for your glory.

Lord, your word is a lantern to our feet
Shine your light upon our path.

We hold before you those who are ill or in any kind of special need . . .
We pray for all who are tormented physically or mentally,
all who feel the strain of caring for someone at home,
however willingly that care is given.
We pray for those coming to terms with a terminal illness –
either their own mortality or someone they love dearly.
May we rejoice in the joy of your saving presence.

Lord, your word is a lantern to our feet
Shine your light upon our path.

We commend to your goodness all who have died . . .
May the light of the gospel fill our hearts with hope in our risen Lord.

Lord, your word is a lantern to our feet
Shine your light upon our path.

We rejoice and join our Alleluias with those of Mark and the whole
company of heaven as we commend ourselves and all people to your
ever present love.

PHILIP AND JAMES, APOSTLES

Festival

1 May

Lord of truth and life
Guide us in your way.

Lord, you are always more ready to satisfy our desires and needs than we
    can ever imagine.
Feed us with your holy Word.
Inspire us with a vision of your glory, that the world may resound with
    your praise.
We give thanks for all who have helped us to become followers
    of your Son.
Give us grace to lead others to find their way to become your disciples.

Lord of truth and life
Guide us in your way.

We pray for all who seek to serve through political office.
We pray for a society at peace with itself,
welcoming of strangers and ready to share the hospitality of the Kingdom.
Give us a hunger and thirst for what is right, for justice and peace.

Lord of truth and life
Guide us in your way.

We pray for all whose hearts are troubled;
for the anxious, the frightened.
We admit the times when we doubt your salvation, that you have a
    place for us.
We pray for all who are spiritually hungry and don't know
    where to trust.
May we recognize your way,
have courage to step out into your truth
and so find your life.

Lord of truth and life
Guide us in your way.

We pray for all who are hungry and thirsty,
for places of famine and drought.
We pray for those struggling on low incomes and beset by debt.
We pray for all tempted to fill their hunger in destructive ways and with
   false hopes;
for all addicted to drugs or who try to satisfy their craving with empty
   relationships.
Give us this day our daily bread, the bread of life.

Lord of truth and life
Guide us in your way.

We pray for all suffering people,
for all afflicted by debilitating diseases
and those who face a diminishing of their faculties.
We pray for those whose hearts break as they watch a loved one in their
   distress . . .
Strengthen our trust in your saving love.

Lord of truth and life
Guide us in your way.

Lord, your Son promised that there is a place for us in your Kingdom.
We give you thanks for all who have gone before us
and now dwell in the mansion of your love . . .
Grant us to share in your celestial banquet.

Lord of truth and life
Guide us in your way.

Rejoicing with Philip and James and the whole company of heaven, we
bring all our prayers to your gracious mercy.

MATTHIAS, APOSTLE

Festival

14 May

Gracious God
Let all peoples praise you.

Lord God, you know our hearts better than we do ourselves,
and in your gracious mercy
chose Matthias to replace Judas as one of the twelve.
We give thanks for the witness of those who travelled with your Son,
who shared his ministry and knew the wonder of his resurrection.
Inspire our hearts to proclaim your transforming love with thanksgiving
   and awe.

Gracious God
Let all peoples praise you.

Lord, you call all to follow you
and bless us with different gifts for the building up of your body, the
   Church.
Hear us as we pray for this Church,
for N our bishop and all whom you call to oversee the ministry of your
   people . . .
With Justus, who was not chosen to apostleship,
we lay before you our ambitions and vocation,
trusting in the providence of your guiding Spirit.

Gracious God
Let all peoples praise you.

Peter sought nominations from the whole community.
We pray for those to whom the responsibility of leadership and
   government is given;
those chosen by vote and those appointed to or born into their office.

May we always remember that all authority owes its true allegiance
  to you.
Guide and uphold them in the challenges and decisions that come before
  them.

Gracious God
Let all peoples praise you.

We pray for all eaten away with jealousy and envy;
any dissatisfied with where they are
or feel they have been passed over for another.
We pray for the embittered and angry;
for any who cannot face their own guilt.
We give thanks for all who help us confront the darkness within.
We bring in our prayers any who cry for your healing touch . . .
Restore your people to wholeness and the freedom that comes through
  trusting in you.

Gracious God
Let all peoples praise you.

As we recall Matthias replacing Judas,
we pray for those who have taken their own lives through depression
or because they cannot live with the knowledge of what they have done.
We pray for all who have died in faith and fear . . .
Lord, your Son delved into the depths of Hades.
Raise us with all the departed to new life in him.

Gracious God
Let all peoples praise you.

In company with Matthias and faithful witnesses throughout the ages, we
offer our prayers before your gracious majesty.

VISIT OF THE BLESSED VIRGIN MARY
TO ELIZABETH

Festival

31 May

Faithful God
Fulfil our longing hearts.

As we join with Mary in magnifying your holy name,
so may we rejoice in your salvation.
We pray for the Church,
giving thanks for all the generations that have blessed you.
We pray for *N* our bishop,
for this community of faith,
and all who leap for joy at the fulfilment of your Word . . .
May we in our own age be faithful witnesses to your love
and teach us to be expectant of your promises.

Faithful God
Fulfil our longing hearts.

We pray for the mighty,
for all who occupy thrones and bear the responsibility of government.
We pray for the lowly,
for all struggling to make ends meet on low incomes or benefits,
all who feel shut out from the corridors of power or influence,
all who cry for justice.
Give us a desire to use the wealth of your bounty
     for the common good.

Faithful God
Fulfil our longing hearts.

We pray for all who have life growing within them,
those pregnant with hope and excitement,
those fearful, frightened and anxious by the changes they are experiencing.

31

We pray for antenatal groups and all who support new or expectant
  parents;
for children's hospitals and neonatal units.
Be with those whose hearts are filled with sadness at being childless.
Bless our families, those who support us and who turn to us for support;
our companions and friends, those with whom we can laugh
  and share news.

Faithful God
Fulfil our longing hearts.

As we sing of your goodness,
we hold before you all for whom our prayers have been asked . . .
Strengthen and uphold them with your gracious love.

Faithful God
Fulfil our longing hearts.

God of our ancestors and descendants,
you hold all life before you.
Hear our prayers for those who have died . . .
Give your peace to hearts that ache with grief
and all who have been carrying the pain for many years.
Grant us to share in your eternal kingdom.

Faithful God
Fulfil our longing hearts.

As we rejoice and exalt you, in fellowship with Blessed Mary and
Elizabeth, we entrust all our prayers to your gracious mercy.

BARNABAS, APOSTLE

Festival

11 June

Generous God
Open our hearts to the gift of your peace.

Merciful God, your love spreads like oil
seeping into the crevices of our crusty exterior.
It finds its way through the narrow gaps to penetrate our tightly pressed
    barriers.
In similar manner you gave grace to your apostle Barnabas to trust Paul
when others clung to fear and suspicion.
Your love through him helped Paul transform
from vicious opponent to determined champion of the gospel.
Inspire us with this charity to accept the second chances we receive
and to be open to offer them to others.

Generous God
Open our hearts to the gift of your peace.

As Barnabas sold all he had so that the proceeds could be held in
    common,
we pray for generosity in our giving to support the mission of the
    Church.
As our hearts are captured for your Kingdom,
so may we transmit this into the currency of action.
We pray for the Church's mission,
for *N* our bishop and all who share with us in proclaiming your love . . .

Generous God
Open our hearts to the gift of your peace.

Christ in glory, before you empires and kingdoms crumble and fall.
At your name every tongue confesses that you are Lord of all.

We pray for those who carry the responsibility that comes with
government.
We pray for those frightened to admit mistakes or to show their
fallibility.
Pour out your Spirit to guide all nations in the ways of peace with
integrity.

Generous God
Open our hearts to the gift of your peace.

Lord, in your Son you shared our frailty and know our weaknesses.
We pray for the ailing
and those whose mortality has moved to the forefront of their minds . . .
Bless us and uphold us with your inbreathing Spirit.

Generous God
Open our hearts to the gift of your peace.

Risen Lord, Barnabas travelled to celebrate and proclaim the hope we
have in you.
In this faith we pray for all who have died . . .
Bring us at the last to share in the new Jerusalem,
where tears are no more and there is life everlasting.

Generous God
Open our hearts to the gift of your peace.

Christ, who came to call sinners to repentance and transform us all in
the image of your glory, we make our prayers in your name.

THE BIRTH OF JOHN THE BAPTIST

Festival

24 June

Blessed be the Lord our God
For we have been redeemed.

Heavenly Father, your prophets have told of your saving love
and you filled John the Baptist with your grace to prepare the way for
    your Son.
Send your Holy Spirit on your Church, that we may find a voice to cry
    out to your praise.
Give us the courage to speak boldly,
to call to repentance and speak the words of salvation,
to turn the hearts of the disobedient to your wisdom.
We pray for N our bishop and all who prepare the way for the
    gospel . . .
May your Church leap for joy at the good news of your Son.

Blessed be the Lord our God
For we have been redeemed.

We pray for those called to the service of high office;
for political leaders and those who direct industry and commerce.
We pray for justice in our dealings with others – legal, social and
    economic;
for all imprisoned for their prophetic stand
and those who face persecution for speaking out against corruption
    and abuse.
We pray for those who look to a different direction
    for our common life,
those with whom we disagree, even those who hate us.
Give us grace to trust in the fulfilment of your promises and to long for
    your Kingdom.
Guide our feet into the way of peace.

Blessed be the Lord our God
For we have been redeemed.

We pray for all who know the joy of life growing within them;
and for those who long for such joy;
for those who cannot conceive or are having difficulty conceiving;
those filled with excitement and any who do not know where to turn.
We pray for new parents, maternity units, and all involved in health care
   for the young.
Praise God for the gift of children,
for their laughter that fills our hearts with joy,
for their eyes of wonder and awe,
for their openness to learn and grow.
May your hand be with them that they may become all that you would
   desire for them.

Blessed be the Lord our God
For we have been redeemed.

We pray for all who sit in darkness and in the shadow of death.
We hold before you all for whom our prayers have been asked . . .
We pray for those with impediments of speech, for speech therapists and
   voice trainers;
for those who are fearful of what to say or how to say it.
We give thanks for the skill of doctors and midwives,
for all who assist in birth and who care for newborns and their mothers.
By your tender mercy may the light of your presence break upon us.

Blessed be the Lord our God
For we have been redeemed.

God of our beginning and our end,
we thank you for revealing in your Son knowledge of your saving love.
We pray for all who have died in both faith and fear . . .
We give thanks for all who have walked before you in holiness and
   righteousness,
whose lives have inspired and drawn us on in our pilgrimage.
May we come to see your salvation.

Blessed be the Lord our God
For we have been redeemed.

As we rejoice and bless your holy name, in union with John the Baptist, Elizabeth and Zechariah, we place the whole of creation before your gracious mercy.

PETER, APOSTLE

Festival

29 June

God of grace, God of mercy
Restore us in your love.

Merciful Lord,
who called impetuous and faltering Peter to follow you,
we thank you that your grace allows your Church
to be built on the rocks of our frailty.
Guide and sustain your Church with your Holy Spirit,
that it may feed and tend your flock.
May our love for you be faithful and true.
Keep our vision focused on your presence,
that we may follow in trust and hope.

God of grace, God of mercy
Restore us in your love.

We pray for all who help unlock the treasures of your Kingdom;
for those who open to us the scriptures;
those who open to us your sacramental presence;
those who open to us the challenge of your justice.
We pray for all bishops and church leaders . . .
those preparing for ordination/recently ordained . . .
We pray for church officers and pastoral carers,
for all ministers of word and sacrament.
May we see Peter's keys opening access to your glory
and ensure that we lock no one out.

God of grace, God of mercy
Restore us in your love.

We pray for those we elect to serve through political office:
in local councils, Parliament, Europe and the United Nations.
We pray for a strengthening of the bonds that unite,

a willingness to listen in differences and conflicts,
that all may be honoured and seek the common good.
We pray for wisdom and integrity in the exercise of power,
for an equal and just sharing of all the earth affords.

God of grace, God of mercy
Restore us in your love.

We pray for our family and friends;
for those closest to us,
and for those we find it difficult to love or who try our patience.
We pray for places of hospitality and refreshment.
We pray for all whose livelihood depends on the seas
and their communities that depend on them;
for the Royal National Lifeboat Institution and coastguards.

God of grace, God of mercy
Restore us in your love.

We hold before you all who are in any need,
physically, psychologically or spiritually . . .
We pray for the dying, the despairing,
for any frightened to be counted as your disciples;
for those facing persecution for their faith.

God of grace, God of mercy
Restore us in your love.

We commend to you all who have died . . .
We pray for the grieving,
any who find it difficult to let go into new life
or who are becoming embittered by a violent or accidental death of a
    loved one.
Unlock the door of our hearts to your saving love.

God of grace, God of mercy
Restore us in your love.

In fellowship with Peter and all the apostles, we rejoice in your
restoring love.

THOMAS, APOSTLE

Festival

3 July

Jesus our way, our truth, our life
Give us your peace.

Risen Lord Jesus,
you stood among your disciples and proclaimed peace.
Your friend Thomas could not believe until he was able to see and
    touch.
We pray for all who find faith hard to grasp
and for those who profess it with an all-consuming exuberance.
We give thanks for our questions, which you make the door to belief
    and understanding.
With you our doubts become the drive to delve more deeply into your
    mystery.
May we trust in your unfailing love that holds us in doubt and in faith.

Jesus our way, our truth, our life
Give us your peace.

We pray for the Church, especially in India, which according to
    tradition was founded by Thomas.
We pray for *N* our bishop and for all with whom we share the name of
    Christ . . .
Fill us with your life-changing Spirit to proclaim the wonder of your
    love.
We pray for a greater understanding and friendship between Christians of
    different traditions.
Give us a bias towards charity when interpreting actions or words that
    seem strange to us.

Jesus our way, our truth, our life
Give us your peace.

We pray for those on whom we place the burden of political office,
and those who readily seek places of honour and responsibility.
We pray for the times we jump in without fully realizing what we are
  getting into.
We pray for all who work long hours
and have little time for reflection or to be with those they love.
We pray for working conditions that honour the whole person
and strengthen the relationships that give us joy and peace.

Jesus our way, our truth, our life
Give us your peace.

We pray for all in whom we see the marks of the cross in their
  suffering;
for those who are crippled with arthritis and who live with discomfort;
for those who don't understand why they can't remember any more
  and are confused;
all who have watched the person they knew diminish or vanish before
  their eyes.
We bring before you in prayer . . .

Jesus our way, our truth, our life
Give us your peace.

Thomas greeted his risen Lord with adoration, calling him 'My Lord and
  my God'.
We commend to your loving care those who have died . . .
Grant us with them a place in your Father's house.

Jesus our way, our truth, our life
Give us your peace.

Rejoicing with Thomas and all the apostles and saints, we entrust all for
whom we pray to your redeeming love.

MARY MAGDALENE, APOSTLE TO THE APOSTLES

Festival

22 July

Lord, you call us by name
And our hearts delight in your praise.

Mary stood weeping, and through her tears heard you call her name.
Inspire your Church with the good news she proclaimed.
May our eyes come to see you with faith
and trust in the fulfilment of your promises.
We pray for all who are sent to ears that are startled
by the message of love and forgiveness.
Give us the courage to account
for the light that is within and among us.

Lord, you call us by name
And our hearts delight in your praise.

We pray for the Church, founded on the rock of apostles, evangelists,
    pastors and teachers;
for the ministry of women,
whose voices have for so long not been heard,
or whose validity has been doubted and questioned;
for those who still feel demeaned or undervalued.
Give us generosity in our stewardship of resources;
a fair sharing to sustain mission and ministry.
We pray for *N* our bishop, for the mission of our diocese, area and
    parish . . .

Lord, you call us by name
And our hearts delight in your praise.

Guide all who are given positions of civic leadership.
Provoke with your Spirit concern and passion for justice

42

and the relief of the weakest peoples of the world and our society.
We pray for those who stand at the margins of power and wealth;
all who make good use of what they have
and the opportunities this affords for the common good.

Lord, you call us by name
And our hearts delight in your praise.

Liberating Lord, hear our prayer for all involved in ministries of
   wholeness and healing.
We pray for all embarrassed by their illness
or who are made to feel unclean;
for those troubled by torments of the mind;
or drawn into ways of life and practices that diminish their worth.
We hold before you those for whom we pray by name or in the silence
   of our hearts . . .

Lord, you call us by name
And our hearts delight in your praise.

We pray for all who stand weeping by a grave;
for those who do not have the body on which to complete their final
   acts of love.
Comfort all whose love in grief makes them want to cling to what
   cannot be held.
We pray for those who have died . . .

Lord, you call us by name
And our hearts delight in your praise.

With the joy of a refreshed encounter with our risen Lord in our hearts,
we commend all creation to your redeeming love.

JAMES, APOSTLE

Festival

25 July

Jesus, servant king
Your Kingdom come, your will be done.

Lord, you called James to leave his fishing boats and follow you.
Give us the willingness to leave everything we know and trust to heed
   your call.
Give us your grace to step out into the unknown,
to die to self that we may live to you.
As James was the first apostle to be martyred,
so we pray for all who suffer for their faith.
We give you thanks for the witness of martyrs through the ages
   and today.

Jesus, servant king
Your Kingdom come, your will be done.

As James and his brother John asked for the places of honour,
give to your Church a heart for service.
We pray for N our bishop . . .
We give thanks for the vision of your glory that inspires and feeds our
   pilgrimage of faith;
that you draw us all to drink of the same cup,
the cup of blessing in the agony of the garden
and the foretaste of the celestial banquet.

Jesus, servant king
Your Kingdom come, your will be done.

We pray for political leaders,
those who scrabble for power
and those who have authority placed on them by others.

Give to all politicians and decision-makers grace to use their power for
the good of all.
We pray for employers and human resources officers,
for small businesses and the self-employed.

Jesus, servant king
Your Kingdom come, your will be done.

As James witnessed your Son's agony in the garden,
we pray for those who are anxious and facing challenges they would
rather avoid.
Give us the strength we need to face the cup we would prefer to be
taken away.
We hold before you all for whom our prayers have been asked,
whatever their need . . .
Give them the grace and comfort of your presence with them.

Jesus, servant king
Your Kingdom come, your will be done.

We commend to your goodness all who have died . . .
We pray for those shocked and disturbed by a sudden death;
those who have died violently and without warning;
those who have died at the hands of terrorism or abusive regimes;
for the disappeared and those who do not have a body to bury.
Heal our grief and bring us to rejoice in your salvation.

Jesus, servant king
Your Kingdom come, your will be done.

In fellowship with James and all the apostles, we rejoice in your
redeeming love.

ANNE AND JOACHIM, PARENTS OF THE BLESSED VIRGIN MARY

Lesser Festival

26 July

God of grace
Fulfil your word.

God of our longing,
through Blessed Mary, daughter of Anne and Joachim,
we see the flowering of grace in the gift of your Son, Jesus Christ.
Keep us expectant with your Word,
filled with hope
and trusting in the fulfilment of your promises.

God of grace
Fulfil your word.

We pray for the Church,
for faith-filled witness to your eternal providence.
We pray for *N* our bishop . . .
May your Church live as those who truly trust in your saving presence.

God of grace
Fulfil your word.

Bless all parents and those who guide the young.
May they help them grow on sure foundations,
equipping them for whatever they may become.
We pray for schools and all places of education,
for youth leaders and all who inspire young people;
for parenting courses and schemes to help those struggling to cope.
We give thanks for the sacrifice of loving parents for their children;
for all that is given without counting the cost.

God of grace
Fulfil your word.

Loving Father, we pray for all who make policies affecting family life;
for those responsible for conditions of employment and our communal
living.
We pray for those who have to adjudicate when relationships break
down;
for family courts and social workers,
for access centres,
and for parents who feel aggrieved by contact arrangements.

God of grace
Fulfil your word.

Lift all whose vision of promise has been dulled
by exhaustion or depressive illness.
Hear our prayer for all who suffer in any way . . .
We give thanks for those whose loving arms embrace anyone
in their need.

God of grace
Fulfil your word.

As we rejoice and exalt in your glory, we commend to you those who
have died . . .
We pray for those who carry the sadness of grief and who long for
comfort in their sorrow.
Teach us to sing the Alleluias of promises fulfilled.

God of grace
Fulfil your word.

Rejoicing in the songs of praise, in union with Anne and Joachim, we
join our prayers with the host of heaven.

THE TRANSFIGURATION OF OUR LORD

Festival

6 August

God of Glory
We will rejoice and be glad in you.

God of our salvation,
as we stand before the throne of grace,
increase in us the vision of your glory,
that we may capture the moment in tents of righteous and holy living.
We pray for *N* our bishop and all your Church . . .
Help us to listen to your eternal Word in Jesus Christ,
that your Church may draw all to enter into the mystery and majesty of
    your presence.

God of Glory
We will rejoice and be glad in you.

Gracious God,
as we enter the cloud of your mystery
help us to choose between the clouds of glory and those of darkness.
On the day when a different, mushroom-shaped cloud
was first seen in conflict over Hiroshima,
help us to use the fruits of science wisely and for the benefit of all your
    creation.
We pray for world leaders, those who determine policies and strategies
    for peace.
Fill our hearts with your love,
that peace may flow like rivers from your holy mountain.

God of Glory
We will rejoice and be glad in you.

God of our Freedom,
as we look on the scene of Jesus standing with Moses and Elijah,

looking to the Exodus to be brought through the cross,
help us to proclaim and work for the liberation that comes through your
  beloved Son.
We pray for those enslaved by economic chains of debt or poverty,
for those bound by addictions and false aspirations.
Give to all the freedom that comes through your glory and your
  salvation.

God of Glory
We will rejoice and be glad in you.

We bring to your mountain of grace
all who are ill, all suffering from limiting diseases
and those who watch as a loved one's faculties are diminishing.
We pray for all whose vision has become clouded by pain and distress.
We pray for all who have lost the mystery and become cynical or
  embittered.
We thank you for those whose sufferings are transfigured
and in their weakness proclaim your glory . . .
Grant us the joy of your saving presence.

God of Glory
We will rejoice and be glad in you.

Hear us, as with hearts of thanks and praise,
we pray for all who now share in a clearer vision of your eternal glory.
We pray for loved ones departed,
for those who have been an inspiration
and any whose memory makes us aware of our need for healing . . .
We pray for all whose grief feels like a cloud of darkness and sadness.
Help us to see through to the glorious and marvellous light of your
  heavenly Kingdom
where we long to share in the company of your heavenly host.

God of Glory
We will rejoice and be glad in you.

Rejoicing with all who have been witnesses to your majesty down the
ages, we offer these and all our prayers to your unfailing goodness.

BARTHOLOMEW, APOSTLE

Festival

24 August

Lord, you know our desires before we ask
Fulfil the promise of your glory.

Lord, you promised that your apostle Bartholomew
   would see heaven opened,
and the angels of God ascending and descending upon the Son of Man.
Open our eyes to the wonders of your love.
Give us faith to know that we are known by you and are precious
   in your sight.
We pray for all who are eaten away by cynicism
and the despising of others and themselves.
Restore in us hope and trust in your saving plan.

Lord, you know our desires before we ask
Fulfil the promise of your glory.

We pray for the Church,
built on the foundation
of your Son's sending out apostles and story-tellers in his name.
We pray for all who proclaim your marvellous presence today.
Send labourers for the harvest
and missionaries for our own age.
We pray for *N* our bishop . . .
Keep us faith-filled and longing for your Kingdom.

Lord, you know our desires before we ask
Fulfil the promise of your glory.

We pray for those who carry the weight of government and political
   leadership.
We pray for all who suffer under the burden of prejudice, persecution
   and hatred,

be it religiously, racially or gender based.
May our justice mirror your justice,
our peace reflect the true peace that passes our understanding.

Lord, you know our desires before we ask
Fulfil the promise of your glory.

We hold in your presence all who are infirm,
wounded or afflicted by any kind of adversity . . .
We pray for those who show us great love,
and for those who approach us with inexplicable hostility.

Lord, you know our desires before we ask
Fulfil the promise of your glory.

We bring before you those who have carried the torch of faith
and now see the greater things promised.
We pray for those we have known and loved who have died . . .
Risen Christ, may we all come to share in your Kingdom.

Lord, you know our desires before we ask
Fulfil the promise of your glory.

In communion with Bartholomew and all the apostles, we commit our
prayers to you through Christ our Lord.

HOLY CROSS DAY

Festival

14 September

Crucified redeemer
We sing your praise.

In the cross of Christ we glory and triumph in this alone.
We pray for the Church,
that it will truly trust in walking the way of the cross
and not in delusions of power and control.
We pray for prophetic leadership;
for N our bishop, for all who preach and inspire faith . . .
May the Church embody dying to self and living to you.

Crucified redeemer
We sing your praise.

We pray for those who sit in the seats of judgement,
for magistrates, judges, and all who administer justice and discipline.
We pray for those who make laws and hold tensions in society.
Give to those in power the courage never to decide that it is expedient
    for one to die
so that prejudice and self-interest remain unchallenged.
Be with the unknown, unnamed who suffer persecution and violence
    each day.

Crucified redeemer
We sing your praise.

Inscribed upon the cross we see your love shining out to all.
We pray for those who expend themselves in love for others
in lives of service and self-sacrifice.
We pray for all who suffer in any way . . .
May we see through the cross that there is no darkness
    that is not touched by your love.

Crucified redeemer
We sing your praise.

We pray for the dying,
for those who keep vigil by their side,
and those who will die alone.
We pray for the departed . . .
Hold before us the cross of glory and the hope of your salvation.

Crucified redeemer
We sing your praise.

Giving glory to Christ, crucified and raised for our salvation, we
commend ourselves and all people to the mighty power of your love.

MATTHEW, APOSTLE AND EVANGELIST

Festival

21 September

God is with us
We praise your holy name.

Generous God,
we commemorate with thanksgiving Matthew's change of heart
and decision to follow you.
We give thanks for the Gospel that bears his name;
for his making known Emmanuel, your presence with us in your Son.
Keep us faithful to our calling and give us the resolve we need
    to follow you.

God is with us
We praise your holy name.

We pray for the Church,
for all ministers of Word and Sacrament;
all pastors and evangelists;
all who proclaim your saving love today.
We pray for *N* our bishop . . .
We pray for all who announce forgiveness to the penitent;
all who search out those others would write off
and who open to them the gateway to mercy and new life.

God is with us
We praise your holy name.

We pray for all tax officials,
those who hold the common purse
and ensure that public services have the funds they need.
We pray for those who create the wealth we enjoy,
for a just and honest stewardship of these resources.
We give thanks for the generosity that finances so many good causes,

those whose sacrificial giving enables the Church's ministry to function
in all parts of the world and our communities.
Guide with your justice all who determine the policies our taxes fund.

God is with us
We praise your holy name.

We pray for those weighed down with financial worries,
those struggling for the staples of life,
and those whose riches cause them anxiety.
Lord, help us all to give to you what belongs to you and to trust in your
    promises.
We pray for those who are ill or whose concerns we carry with us . . .

God is with us
We praise your holy name.

As we long for the things of heaven, we pray for all who have died . . .
Risen Lord, bless those who mourn,
that they may know the comfort of your presence with us.

God is with us
We praise your holy name.

Rejoicing that your Kingdom has come near to us in Christ our Lord,
with Matthew and all the apostles, we raise this anthem of praise
to your glory.

MICHAEL AND ALL ANGELS

Festival

29 September

Bless the Lord all you his host
Praise his holy name.

God of visions and dreams,
open our hearts to your heavenly glory.
We rejoice that in Christ the victory already is.
Be with us in the struggles of life;
keep us from succumbing to evil.
Help us to see the holiness of the ground on which we all stand;
that we are before the gate of heaven.
We join our prayers with the host of heaven.

Bless the Lord all you his host
Praise his holy name.

God of awe and wonder,
let your glory loose on your Church.
Transform it in your love.
Renew it in confidence in your power and your hold on your creation.
Bless and guide *N* our bishop and all who exercise spiritual leadership . . .
Increase in us a sense of awe and worship for your name.

Bless the Lord all you his host
Praise his holy name.

God of messengers and heralds,
open the hearts of all to your words of healing and peace.
We pray for those who seek to interpret the world in the light of your
    good news
and who challenge with the prophetic voice.
We pray for all who lead nations;
for local councils and community groups;

for all who engage with the political struggle for justice
  and the common good.

Bless the Lord all you his host
Praise his holy name.

God our strength and stay in adversity,
we pray for all embattled with personal conflicts
or oppressions of mind, body or spirit . . .
We pray for all whose vision of glory feels impeded.
Help us to recognize your love in our frailty
and send on all for whom we pray your healing touch.

Bless the Lord all you his host
Praise his holy name.

God our protector at the hour of our death,
we pray for those whose lives are drawing to a close,
and for those who have died . . .
Open to all the gate of heaven, that we may truly be inheritors of your
  salvation.

Bless the Lord all you his host
Praise his holy name.

Standing before the throne of righteousness, with Michael and All Angels
and the whole host of heaven, we commend these and all our prayers to
your eternal goodness.

LUKE, EVANGELIST

Festival

18 October

Lord, we come before your presence
Heal us with your word of life.

Loving Lord, we give you thanks for your evangelist Luke,
whose Gospel sets our imaginations on fire with the good news
   of your Son.
We pray for all who translate the scriptures,
for theologians who interpret their message
and preachers who make the words come alive to feed our souls.
We pray for those with the gift of story-telling,
for dramatists and choreographers who arouse the well of our thoughts.

Lord, we come before your presence
Heal us with your word of life.

We pray for the Church,
for our inheritance of faith and those who labour for the gospel today.
We pray for *N* our bishop . . .
Generous God, your salvation is for all.
Teach us to embrace all people with the same love we see in your Son.

Lord, we come before your presence
Heal us with your word of life.

Lord, Luke wrote for an official named Theophilus.
We pray for those who hold temporal power;
for decision-makers and all who shape the direction of our common life.
We pray for spiritual advisers and chaplains to rulers,
members of parliament and councils;
all whose wisdom and insight is sought,
who make connections between your gospel and the issues of
   government.

Lord, we come before your presence
Heal us with your word of life.

Heavenly Father, your beloved physician offered cures for ailments of
  mind, body and spirit.
We pray for all involved in healing,
for doctors and nurses, complementary practitioners,
and all who open up wholeness and restoration to broken people.
We pray for hospital chaplains and visitors;
for ancillary staff and all involved in the management of health care
  provision.
We pray for patients and their families and friends.
Among those for whom our prayers have been asked . . .

Lord, we come before your presence
Heal us with your word of life.

Lord, Luke presents us with the drama of your salvation in your Son
  Jesus Christ.
We commend to you all who have died . . .
Refresh the hope you hold before us in the resurrection of Christ from
  the dead.

Lord, we come before your presence
Heal us with your word of life.

In communion with Luke and the whole household of God, we entrust
all your people to your eternal goodness.

SIMON AND JUDE, APOSTLES

Festival

28 October

God of truth and hope
We raise our prayer with thanksgiving.

Eternal God, you hold the whole world in your loving providence.
We thank you that your Son called a rich diversity of men and women
to be his apostles and proclaim his name.
As we commemorate Simon and Jude,
refresh our vision
and give us a clear sense of your will.
Give us humility to change our direction where we are straying
or pursuing a destructive course.

God of truth and hope
We raise our prayer with thanksgiving.

We pray for the Church,
founded on the witness of the apostles and faithful men and women
    down the ages.
We pray for this church . . .
for *N* our bishop . . .
Guide and strengthen with your living presence all who proclaim the
    name of Christ.

God of truth and hope
We raise our prayer with thanksgiving.

Simon, the Zealot, belonged to a group of nationalist resistance fighters.
We pray for all who take up the struggle for freedom.
Keep us from damaging the justice we seek by the means we employ;
preserve us from being eaten away by hatred
and consumed with violence.
We pray for all who hold positions of political leadership and
    government.

God of truth and hope
We raise our prayer with thanksgiving.

We hold before you all for whom our prayers have been asked
and those who have no one to pray for them . . .
We pray for all who feel their cause is lost or whose grip on hope has
   been weakened;
for the suicidal and depressed,
the deeply anxious and all troubled by disturbances of the mind.
Bless the work of the Samaritans and all who stay with those in any kind
   of distress.

God of truth and hope
We raise our prayer with thanksgiving.

We remember with thankful hearts
those we have known and who have died . . .
We pray for all who feel lost in their grief
and those who need to rebuild their lives in hope and trust.
Renew our faith in our risen Lord.

God of truth and hope
We raise our prayer with thanksgiving.

Lord, as citizens of your household, rejoicing in fellowship with Simon
and Jude, we place ourselves and all creation in the hands of your
redeeming love.

ALL SAINTS

Principal Feast

1 November

Sanctifying God
We exalt your name.

Sacred God, you are the Holy One,
the source of life and the fountain of our hope.
Pour out your Spirit on your Church;
breathe into it the fire of your love.
Set us free to sing your praises, that as we share your life
so we may taste and see your gracious love.

Sanctifying God
We exalt your name.

We give thanks for all your saints throughout the ages;
for the lives of men and women sanctified by the power of your
    presence.
We pray for the saints of the church in this place,
all whose lives proclaim the wonders of your saving love.
We pray for *N* our bishop and all Christian men and women . . .
Bless and guide your children, that we may be built into living temples
    of your peace.

Sanctifying God
We exalt your name.

We hold up before your throne of grace those whom we elect to lead
    and govern.
We pray for peace with justice;
for a healing of conflicts and hatreds that tear apart the lives of so many;
for a just and fair sharing of all the earth affords.
Give us a humble heart,

that the simplicity of our living may proclaim our trust in your
   providential care
and the glory of your Kingdom.

Sanctifying God
We exalt your name.

With the voice of praise and thanksgiving we place our trust in your
   unfailing love.
We pray for all in any kind of need . . .
Transform us by your grace and lead us to rejoice and be glad in you.

Sanctifying God
We exalt your name.

Looking to the holy city, the new Jerusalem, when all has passed away,
we commend to your mercy all who have died . . .
Bless those who mourn, that they may be comforted,
wipe away the tears of grief,
and let us rejoice and be glad in your salvation.

Sanctifying God
We exalt your name.

Rejoicing in the great cloud of witnesses that surround us and with
whom we share our citizenship of heaven, we commit ourselves and all
creation to your eternal protection.

ALL SOULS – ALL SAINTSTIDE
COMMEMORATION OF THE DEPARTED

Lesser Festival

2 November

Lord of life and hope
We trust in your saving love.

We join our prayers with the saints in glory.
Seeing that we share in a communion with a great cloud of witnesses,
lift our hearts to the heavenly places.
Fill us with a vision of your eternal splendour
and draw us deeper into the reign of your Kingdom.
We give thanks for all who have served here in the past,
for the inheritance of faith and prayer.
May we be faithful witnesses to your light and hope
    in our own generation.
We pray for *N* our bishop and all with whom we share the name of
    Christ . . .

Lord of life and hope
We trust in your saving love.

Your Kingdom is an everlasting Kingdom.
We pray for those who have responsibility of government for a while
    on earth;
for justice and peace throughout the world;
for local councillors,
for our MP and all who sit in the high court of Parliament.
Bless all people of good will with whom we can work to transform the
    structures of society.

Lord of life and hope
We trust in your saving love.

We hold before you all for whom our prayers have been asked . . .
We pray for all who despair or have lost confidence in the future;

for those whose faculties are fading or whose spirit is sapped.
Give to them your healing grace and sustaining presence.

Lord of life and hope
We trust in your saving love.

Confident of Christ's victory on the cross,
we remember in love all who have died
and all whose names we bring to be commemorated today . . .
May we come to share in the eternal banquet of your Son
    Jesus Christ.
Give us thankful hearts for his redeeming love.

Lord of life and hope
We trust in your saving love.

We pray for all who carry the pain of grief daily in their hearts;
for all who are lonely;
for those traumatized by what they have seen.
We pray for parents who ache with the loss of a child;
all whose grief has been reopened by a recent event;
for all whose memory needs healing,
or for whom a death begins a painful rediscovery,
as well as those thankful for lives shared.
May the light of your Kingdom shine in every dark place.

Lord of life and hope
We trust in your saving love.

Rejoicing in communion with all your saints, we entrust all people to
your saving love.

REMEMBRANCE – ALL SAINTSTIDE

Special Commemoration

11 November/Second Sunday of November

Lord of all
Give us your peace.

Creator God,
you hold the world in its course
and love everything you have made.
You are the beginning and the end,
the one in whom all people are joined as one family.
Forgive our warring and the conflicts that tear us apart.

Lord of all
Give us your peace.

God of compassion,
your Son sought refuge from Herod's tyranny.
Look with mercy on all who have been displaced by wars and conflicts.
Open our hearts to the plight of refugees
and help us to welcome with hospitality the stranger in need.

Lord of all
Give us your peace.

Sovereign God,
all authority owes true allegiance to you.
Guide those who lead the nations of the world in the paths of peace
    with justice.
Bless those who make peace
and strengthen the bonds that unite in a commonwealth.

Lord of all
Give us your peace.

Almighty God,
whose Son gave himself for love of our love,
we hold before you all who have given themselves
for the protection and security of others;
for acts of bravery and disciplined restraint;
for acts of humanity amid great bloodshed.

Lord of all
Give us your peace.

Loving Lord,
your Son restored to wholeness and health
those who called on him in their need.
Look with mercy and compassion on all who bear the scars of warfare –
emotionally, physically and spiritually.
We pray for those who remember because they cannot forget
and are haunted in the night by what they have seen.

Lord of all
Give us your peace.

Living Lord,
your Son triumphed over the cruelty of death on the cross for our
    redemption.
We lay before you all who have died at the hands of violence and
    war . . .

Silence

Comfort all who mourn and at the last trumpet call bring us every one
    to rise in Christ.

Lord of all
Give us your peace.

Looking to the coming of your Kingdom, on earth as it is in heaven, we
present before you our prayers for all people.

CECILIA, MARTYR
PATRON SAINT OF MUSICIANS, *c.* AD 230

Lesser Festival

22 November

Sing to the Lord, all the earth
Worship the Lord in the beauty of holiness.

Heavenly Father, your love draws us close and bids us welcome.
You reach out in your Son and make space for us in your
   heavenly home.
We give you thanks for the hospitality of Cecilia,
for providing a place for your fledgling Church to gather.
Help us to set aside space for you in our busy lives,
to worship and adore.

Sing to the Lord, all the earth
Worship the Lord in the beauty of holiness.

We give thanks for church musicians;
for composers, directors of choirs,
and all who combine in harmony to sing of your glory.
We pray for organists and instrumentalists,
whose music lifts our worship with joyful sounds.
We pray for the work of the Royal School of Church Music;
for all who promote music-making and train new musicians.

Sing to the Lord, all the earth
Worship the Lord in the beauty of holiness.

We pray for the Church,
for *N* our bishop . . .
We pray for any whose worship costs them dear;
for any who, like Cecilia, bravely allow a place for your praises
   to be sung.
Refresh your Church with the music of heaven.

Sing to the Lord, all the earth
Worship the Lord in the beauty of holiness.

We pray for all on whom we lay the burden of leadership and
government.
May the jubilance of our praise inspire unity and break down the barriers
that divide.
We pray for all who have forgotten how to sing
and how to wonder at the mystery of the world you have made.

Sing to the Lord, all the earth
Worship the Lord in the beauty of holiness.

We hold before your tender compassion any weighed down by
afflictions and pains . . .
Send your healing Spirit to open their hearts to your presence in their
suffering.

Sing to the Lord, all the earth
Worship the Lord in the beauty of holiness.

We commend to your goodness all who have died . . .
We pray for those who have given their lives for their faith
and any facing the prospect of martyrdom as the cost of their worship.
Fulfil in all your children the promises of your saving love.

Sing to the Lord, all the earth
Worship the Lord in the beauty of holiness.

Rejoicing in communion with Cecilia and all your saints and martyrs
throughout the ages, we place our trust in your unceasing love.

ANDREW, APOSTLE
PATRON SAINT OF SCOTLAND

Festival

30 November

Lord, we would see Jesus
Show us your peace.

Standing near the shore of Galilee,
Andrew heard the call to follow.
Your Son promised that henceforth he would fish for people.
We pray for the missionary work of the Church,
for mission societies and a concern that extends beyond all boundaries,
    national, cultural and racial.
As we preach, so may we learn
and discover more of the bounty of your love.

Lord, we would see Jesus
Show us your peace.

We pray for the Church;
for churches founded by Andrew and those named after him.
We pray for *N* our bishop,
for the ancient patriarchate of Constantinople, founded by Andrew,
    and for a greater understanding and fellowship between
    denominations . . .
Refresh us with zeal for your gospel.

Lord, we would see Jesus
Show us your peace.

On this their national day, we pray for our brothers and sisters in
    Scotland.
We pray for the Scottish Parliament;
for those who represent the people in all tiers of government.
We pray for those involved in industry and commerce,

for those who administer our financial institutions
and any whose income has been adversely affected by losses beyond their
    means.
We pray for all who harvest natural resources such as fossil fuels,
and those exploring renewable energy sources.
Make us wise stewards of your goodness.

Lord, we would see Jesus
Show us your peace.

We hold before you all in need of sustenance and refreshment:
the hungry, the thirsty;
all exhausted or at the limits of their endurance . . .
Strengthen and uphold all who call on you.

Lord, we would see Jesus
Show us your peace.

We commend to your saving presence those who have died . . .
Grant them to share in your eternal Kingdom.

Lord, we would see Jesus
Show us your peace.

Rejoicing in union with Andrew and all the apostles, we place these
prayers before your redeeming love.

O SAPIENTIA
THE GREAT 'O'S: THE ADVENT ANTIPHONS

Eight days before Christmas

From 17 December

Come to our salvation
Come, Lord Jesus.

O Wisdom,
whose Word brings all into being
and whose Spirit brings life and peace,
come upon us with your potency.
Inspire our vision and make us expectant
for more than we would otherwise dare dream possible.

Come to our salvation
Come, Lord Jesus.

O Adonai,
Master, Lord of all,
we bow before the magnificence of your holy name.
Forgive us when we abuse it or misuse it
in our speech and through our actions.
Make us worthy to stand before the fire of your presence
made manifest.

Come to our salvation
Come, Lord Jesus.

O Root of Jesse,
who was and is and is to come.
Graft into our hearts true love for you,
that loving you we may serve you
and follow you through joys and sorrows,
strains and celebrations,
doubts and convictions.

72

Come to our salvation
Come, Lord Jesus.

O Key of David,
unlock the door to our hearts.
Shine your light into the depths of our secret places.
Transform our motives and desires,
our plans and striving
for the glory of your Kingdom.

Come to our salvation
Come, Lord Jesus.

O Dayspring,
dawning from the dwelling of God,
reveal the promise of the new day.
Bless us with the gift you hold before us
and keep us in your saving love.

Come to our salvation
Come, Lord Jesus.

O King of the Nations,
the one to whom all authority owes true allegiance,
be with all in high office.
Let your justice flow,
your peace reign,
your liberating Word unbind the chains of deceit and oppression.

Come to our salvation
Come, Lord Jesus.

O Emmanuel,
long expected and looked for,
be present among us.
In the darkness let your light shine,
bringing hope to the despairing,
encouragement to those in danger of losing heart,
and life to all who walk through the shadow of death.

Come to our salvation
Come, Lord Jesus.

As we prepare to celebrate the glory of your coming among us in the child of Bethlehem, so may we be found ready to meet him when he comes in glory.

CHRISTMAS EVE
CRIB SERVICE

Principal Feast

24 December

Jesus, Saviour
Hear the prayers of your people.

Jesus, Son of the most high,
on this night, angels sang to announce your birth.
May our hearts be filled with the joy and hope you bring.

Jesus, Saviour
Hear the prayers of your people.

We pray for all parents and children.
Fill our homes with your love and peace.
We pray for all whose home life is troubled,
or who will be separated from someone they love this Christmas.

Jesus, Saviour
Hear the prayers of your people.

We pray for all who are spending this Christmas in a hospital or a
    hospice;
for those who are ill or dying.
May the hope Jesus brings give us all the joy of your salvation.

Jesus, Saviour
Hear the prayers of your people.

As there was no room in the inn,
we pray for all who are homeless or fearing eviction.
As the Holy Family fled Herod's anger,
we pray for all who have been made refugees by warfare
    or fear of danger.

Jesus, Saviour
Hear the prayers of your people.

We give thanks for your love shown in your gift to us in Jesus.
May we show this thanks in lives that try to follow him every day.

Jesus, Saviour
Hear the prayers of your people.

Uniting our prayers with the host of heaven, we rejoice in your
saving love.

CHRISTMAS DAY

Principal Feast

25 December

Glory to God in the highest
And peace to his people on earth.

With the shepherds we come before your Son to worship and adore.
To the Lamb of God we offer our praise.
We thank you for the greatest gift of all, the gift of yourself in your Son.
Fill us, gracious God, with the life and love of your presence.

Glory to God in the highest
And peace to his people on earth.

As there was no room for the Son of Man at his birth,
we pray for all who have no room in their Christmas for Jesus today.
Forgive us the times we ignore you or push you to the margins of our
    living.

Glory to God in the highest
And peace to his people on earth.

Jesus, you shared the life of a home with Mary and Joseph.
We pray for all children and parents.
Give us thankful hearts for the tokens of love exchanged.
As the Christchild was wrapped in swaddling bands,
we give thanks for the places that wrap us in love
and teach us to honour and care.

Glory to God in the highest
And peace to his people on earth.

We pray for all for whom this day brings sadness or tears;
for those separated from someone they love,
those who carry grief within them,

those breaking under strains they endure.
Kindle in our hearts the good news of great joy
    announced by the angels.

Glory to God in the highest
And peace to his people on earth.

As we celebrate the birth of the Prince of Peace,
we pray for all places of hatred and strife,
places of warfare and violence.
We pray for those with courage to risk peace-making,
for those who dare to seek the healing of conflicts and deep injuries.
Unite us in your Son into a commonwealth of peace and justice.

Glory to God in the highest
And peace to his people on earth.

Uniting our prayers with the host of heaven, we rejoice in your
saving love.

STEPHEN, FIRST MARTYR

Festival

26 December

God of grace and power
Show us your glory.

Servant King, your apostles chose Stephen
to be one who attended to the needs of the saints of the early Church.
Give us a willingness to share one another's burdens,
to relieve hunger and want.
We pray for Crisis and all who give shelter to the homeless at Christmas.

God of grace and power
Show us your glory.

Before he was martyred, Stephen gazed into heaven and saw your glory.
Inspire your Church today with a vision of your heavenly splendour.
Give to all who profess your name courage to be counted as one of your
    number,
and to give an account for the hope that is within them.
We pray for N our bishop . . .
We pray for all whose witness leads them to martyrdom today.

God of grace and power
Show us your glory.

False witnesses were stirred up against Stephen.
We pray for all who uphold justice;
for political leaders and all who hold public office.
Remembering that the coats of those who stoned Stephen were laid at
    Saul's feet,
who later became an apostle for the building up of your Church,
we pray for those whose hearts are hardened and whose ears are covered.

God of grace and power
Show us your glory.

Lord, whose compassion never ceases,
we pray for all who are spending this Christmas in hospital or a hospice;
for all who have been touched by tragedy,
and for whom this season heightens their pain.
We pray for those who don't know how they will pay for gifts they
    have bought on credit;
for the anxious and depressed;
for any whose isolation seems greater at this time,
and for the work of the Samaritans who are there for them . . .

God of grace and power
Show us your glory.

At the hour of his death, Stephen commended his spirit to your Son.
We pray for all nearing the hour of their death and for those who have
    died . . .
Righteous One, open the heavens to receive our spirits.

God of grace and power
Show us your glory.

Placing our hope and trust in your eternal goodness, with Stephen the
first martyr and all the saints and apostles, we commend our spirits
to you.

JOHN, APOSTLE AND EVANGELIST

Festival

27 December

The Word was made flesh
We behold your glory.

Jesus, our way, our truth, our life,
we give you thanks for calling John to follow you;
for the Gospel that bears his name;
for the riches of his testimony,
and the inspired word he gives us.
Open our eyes that we too may see and believe in your beloved Son.

The Word was made flesh
We behold your glory.

Jesus, Good Shepherd,
we pray for the Church founded on your apostles and evangelists.
We pray for N our bishop and all who lead the Church today . . .
Nourish us and all your people with the true bread of life.

The Word was made flesh
We behold your glory.

Jesus, Light of the World,
we pray for all who come to you in the night of worries
and the weight of high office;
for all political leaders,
and those who exercise power and influence over world affairs.
Shine the light of your love to illumine the path of peace and justice.

The Word was made flesh
We behold your glory.

Standing at the foot of the cross,
John endured the agony of the garden through to the end.
We pray for all going through a vale of tears,
for those looking for healing and release,
for those watching and waiting by the side of someone they love . . .
Turn our cries of pain into songs of joy.

The Word was made flesh
We behold your glory.

Jesus, our Resurrection and our Life, we pray for all who have died . . .
Be with those who weep and raise us to the life of your beloved.

The Word was made flesh
We behold your glory.

Rejoicing in fellowship with John and all the beloved in glory, we commend our prayers to your redeeming love.

HOLY INNOCENTS

Festival

28 December

Lord, save us and rescue us
Your Son brings light to our darkness.

On this fourth day of celebrating the light of Christ,
we gaze into the darkness that is the slaughter of innocents.
We shudder at the evil that human beings are capable of committing.
How much we would like to believe that those who commit such
    depravity are less than human,
so much more the horror of our shared humanity disturbs us.
O God, why?

Lord, save us and rescue us
Your Son brings light to our darkness.

Today the laughter is silenced,
the toys lie undisturbed,
the tidiness and quietness of the house is unbearable.
Today we endure the pain that is silent
and the screams that cannot be hushed or shut out.
We pray for all who have known the inconsolable grief of a child being
    murdered or abused.

Lord, save us and rescue us
Your Son brings light to our darkness.

We pray for those who have committed unspeakable evil,
who are hated and despised by angry crowds.
We pray for all who work with them in prisons,
the probation service,
on treatment and after-care programmes.
We pray for those whose guilt is hard to bear;
for their families and friends who have had to face the unpalatable,
whose own screams are often not heard.

Lord, save us and rescue us
Your Son brings light to our darkness.

Holy Child, you came to redeem and to save,
we pray for the Church,
for its ministry of pronouncing forgiveness to the penitent,
healing for the injured,
and salvation open to all.
We pray for *N* our bishop and all ministers of reconciliation . . .
Give us courage to defend the vulnerable and to love the unlovable.

Lord, save us and rescue us
Your Son brings light to our darkness.

As we recall Joseph protecting the infant Jesus by their flight to Egypt,
we pray for all who act to ensure the security and well-being of children
and those at risk.
We pray for social services, health workers, family members and the
courts.
Guide and bless policy-makers and all who shape our common life.

Lord, save us and rescue us
Your Son brings light to our darkness.

On this day of light shining in deep darkness,
we are hushed, subdued by mixed emotions of terror and praise,
fear and gratitude.
With the wise men returning by another route,
open to us a new path of hope and trust in your Son.

2

Principal Feasts and Festivals with Variable Dates

———◆———

THE BAPTISM OF CHRIST

Principal Feast

First Sunday of Epiphany

Lord, you delight in your beloved
We see your salvation.

Heavenly Father,
the crowds flocked to John at the Jordan to be baptized
and prepared for your Kingdom.
We pray for all who long for you and seek after righteousness.
We pray for imaginative ways to make connections
with everyday lives and aspirations;
for those who translate church language and practice
into the vernacular of our living.

Lord, you delight in your beloved
We see your salvation.

Lord, Jesus stepped forward from amid the crowd
and inaugurated his ministry through the water of baptism
and the anointing of the Spirit.
We pray for all who are baptized in his name;
for those preparing for baptism;
for parents celebrating the gift of their child.
We pray for all godparents and the influence and support they offer.

We pray for the Church, the community of the baptized,
for N our bishop and all who name themselves after Christ . . .
Strengthen and confirm us in the same Spirit that descended like a dove.

Lord, you delight in your beloved
We see your salvation.

Lord, your Kingdom makes other kingdoms nervous.
We pray for all who exercise power,
whose decisions affect the lives of the powerless.
We pray for community leaders and representatives of the people;
for all levels of government – local, national and international.
Bind us together as children of the same heavenly Father.

Lord, you delight in your beloved
We see your salvation.

We pray for all who seek relief from distress of the mind, body or
    spirit . . .
We pray for those racked by doubt or despair,
any who find it difficult to have faith or to be hopeful.
Comfort and heal with your prevailing Spirit.

Lord, you delight in your beloved
We see your salvation.

With thankful hearts, we commend to you all who have died . . .
As we pass through the waters of death, so may we rise to new life in
    Christ our Lord.

Lord, you delight in your beloved
We see your salvation.

United in fellowship with all baptized in your name, we commend all
for whom we pray to your gracious mercy.

ASH WEDNESDAY

Principal Feast

Make us hear of joy and gladness
Sustain us with your bountiful Spirit.

In the loneliness of the wilderness,
your Son confronted the torment of evil.
He endured hunger and thirst
and sought only after righteousness.
He was offered easy solutions,
but chose the way of the cross for our redemption.
As we journey through this holy season of Lent,
renew within us your call and our resolve to follow.

Make us hear of joy and gladness
Sustain us with your bountiful Spirit.

Lord, you hold out to us a treasure that cannot be destroyed
or taken away by the envy of others.
We pray for all renewing their faith during this season;
those exploring your gospel for the first time or with fresh eyes;
those preparing for baptism and confirmation.
We pray for N our bishop and all who dedicate themselves to following
 the Way . . .

Make us hear of joy and gladness
Sustain us with your bountiful Spirit.

Heavenly Father, your Son gave up all power to share fully in our
 humanity;
the Creator became as the created to scoop us into the divine.
We pray for those who cling to power;
for those who use their position for the common good,
who even risk losing everything rather than abandon principles deeply
 and nobly held.
We pray for those oppressed and crying out for liberation;

87

for the hungry who call for bread;
for the homeless who long for shelter.

Make us hear of joy and gladness
Sustain us with your bountiful Spirit.

In entering the wilderness, the city and the seashore,
your Son showed that nowhere is beyond your reach.
On the way between places, healing was freely given;
by the well, salvation announced;
in the market place, stones exchanged for the bread of forgiveness.
We pray for all who cry for release from whatever holds them captive;
for the sick, and all of us in our need of your healing touch today . . .
As we are marked with your cross,
so may we know within us your release and blessing.

Make us hear of joy and gladness
Sustain us with your bountiful Spirit.

Through the waters of baptism we die to sin and rise to new life in
    Christ.
We pray for all who have died . . .
Lord, by your cross and resurrection you have redeemed the world.
Renew our trust in this hope
and bring us at the last with all your people
to share in your eternal banquet of praise.

Make us hear of joy and gladness
Sustain us with your bountiful Spirit.

Holy God, holy and immortal,
in the power of the Spirit we make our prayer through your Christ.

MAUNDY THURSDAY

Principal Feast

Jesus, be exalted above the heavens
Let your glory be over all the earth.

On this night,
your Son shared in a meal with his closest friends
and inaugurated the great thanksgiving feast of the Eucharist.
As we break the bread, so may we feed on him who is the bread of life.
As we drink the cup, so may we participate in a foretaste of your
    Kingdom.

Jesus, be exalted above the heavens
Let your glory be over all the earth.

On this night,
your Son took water and a bowl to wash his disciples' feet.
Teach us to accept the loving service of others;
never to abuse it or take it for granted.
May we follow his example in humility and without thought of reward.

Jesus, be exalted above the heavens
Let your glory be over all the earth.

On this night,
your Son prayed in agony in the garden.
May we watch with those who endure the dark night of the soul.
Be with all who pray for the removal of a cup they find hard to bear,
and yet also pray for your will to be done.

Jesus, be exalted above the heavens
Let your glory be over all the earth.

On this night,
your Son was betrayed with a kiss.
We pray for all whose intimacy is abused,

whose trust is destroyed,
or who are placed in the hands of those
who regard them as expendable for their own ends.

Jesus, be exalted above the heavens
Let your glory be over all the earth.

On this night,
your Son was denied by those who had sworn that they would
    die with him
and for him.
Forgive us the times we make promises we cannot keep
or falter when the going proves too hard for us.

Jesus, be exalted above the heavens
Let your glory be over all the earth.

On this night,
your Son endured a false trial.
We pray for all who cry and struggle for justice;
for those silenced by oppressive regimes;
for the disappeared and the disenfranchised.

Jesus, be exalted above the heavens
Let your glory be over all the earth.

Lord, we prepare to journey with you to your cross and resurrection.
We offer these prayers in your name.

GOOD FRIDAY

Principal Feast

Jesus, Saviour of the world
We shall glorify your name.

Standing before the high priest,
your Son made no attempt to deceive or to hide his words and actions.
We pray for all afraid to be open about their intentions or deeds.
We pray for those who fear that their words will be distorted by the
 unscrupulous;
for any who fear truth and being open.

Jesus, Saviour of the world
We shall glorify your name.

Standing bound before Pilate and the crowd,
your Son announced his Kingdom to come,
and the ruler of Palestine faced the Ruler of all.
We pray for those bound by fear of political repercussions;
for those who wash their hands of justice
and collude with the destruction of the innocent.
We pray for all who sit in judgement,
and who must protect those the crowd would lynch.

Jesus, Saviour of the world
We shall glorify your name.

Standing against the whipping post,
your Son was mocked and scourged.
We pray for those who are battered
and endure violence in secret.
We pray for any mocked for their faith
or for the stand they take.

Jesus, Saviour of the world
We shall glorify your name.

91

Standing, struggling under the weight of the cross,
your Son bore our sins and carried our transgressions.
We pray for all made scapegoats for others' offences;
for those easily blamed and those unjustly pilloried for mistakes more
   widely caused.
We pray for victims of false witness and of slander.

Jesus, Saviour of the world
We shall glorify your name.

Standing at the foot of the cross,
Mary and John watched your Son die.
We pray for all who bear the heartbreak of grief.
We pray for the dying and those who have died.
Jesus, remember us in your Kingdom.

Jesus, Saviour of the world
We shall glorify your name.

Lord, by the sacred wounds of your Son, by his death and passion, open
to us the gates of your heavenly city. In this confidence we make our
prayers to you.

EASTER DAY

Principal Feast

Lord of life
Raise us in your Son.

In the silence of the night,
when all lay still and the grave seemed cold and lifeless,
your radiant love broke free and raised your Son.
From nothing your Spirit brought forth life at the beginning of creation.
From the absence of all senses you restored all that had been lost and
    more.
May this astounding news fill our hearts with awe and wonder at your
    saving love.

Lord of life
Raise us in your Son.

In the bright light and spring freshness of early morning,
Mary came to the tomb with oil and spices
to complete that which seemed unfinished.
Startled at what she found,
she dared not even dream anything other than the horror of desecration.
Called by name, she abandoned restraint and flung herself at your raised
    Christ.
May our hearts likewise spring with delight at the new life you give.

Lord of life
Raise us in your Son.

In the gloom of mourners comforting one another, unable to face
    breakfast,
Mary, breathless and bubbling with the excitement of her discovery,
confused the disciples with news of your resurrection.
We pray for the Church, charged with this incredible message.
We pray for N our bishop and all who seek to live in the light of your
    risen Son . . .

May all Christians discover afresh
enthusiasm and excitement for the good news your Son brings.

Lord of life
Raise us in your Son.

In the corridors of power,
news of the empty tomb had to be suppressed and re-spun
to prevent what could not be controlled.
Overcome and destroy the hold of death,
in whatever guise it appears, with the eruption of your new life.
We pray for all who sit on thrones and the seats of government.

Lord of life
Raise us in your Son.

In the house, with doors locked to keep the unknown at bay,
Thomas refused to believe what seemed to him an idle tale,
until sight and touch found a voice in him to proclaim his Lord and
    God.
We hold before you our doubts and fears, our faltering faith.
We pray for all whose confidence in your resurrection
is shaken by sickness or suffering,
as well as those who find a voice to sing your praise . . .
May the wounds of Christ,
transformed in glory,
give comfort and hope.

Lord of life
Raise us in your Son.

In the boat on the sea, the disciples failed to catch anything in the night.
At dawn, with the call of your Son,
a harvest beyond their imagining overwhelmed them.
As we pray for those who have died
we entrust them to him who prepares for us more than we could ever
    imagine . . .
Raise us all to live with you for ever.

Lord of life
Raise us in your Son.

Christ who died is risen. **Alleluia.**
We join our prayers and praise with the whole creation
as we make this our song. **Alleluia. Amen.**

ASCENSION OF OUR LORD

Principal Feast

Be exalted, O God, above the heavens
Let your glory be over all the earth.

King of kings and Lord of lords,
we bow before your throne of grace.
Raised to reign in glory,
you bring to completion all that you have begun to work in creation.
Risen Lord Jesus, rule in our hearts and lives;
inspire us to seek your Kingdom above all and in all.

Be exalted, O God, above the heavens
Let your glory be over all the earth.

Suffering and exalted servant,
may your Church follow your example in ways of loving service;
may our wills be subject to the power of your gospel.
We pray for *N* our bishop . . .
Help us to make disciples of all nations
and to allow no other objects of worship but your eternal name.

Be exalted, O God, above the heavens
Let your glory be over all the earth.

We pray for the kingdoms of this world,
for those to whom we give the responsibility of government.
May they recognize that all authority is ultimately subject to your just
    and gentle rule.
Grant us peace with justice,
the true freedom that seeks the good of all.

Be exalted, O God, above the heavens
Let your glory be over all the earth.

God of glory,
we pray for our homes, for our communities.

May we set our lives on the firm foundations of your promises.
We pray for all who inspire us with a spirit of discipleship,
with the desire to follow in the way of your Son.
May your Kingdom come, your will be done.

Be exalted, O God, above the heavens
Let your glory be over all the earth.

Eternal Lord, look with compassion on those who are ill in mind, body
  or spirit . . .
Strengthen with your Holy Spirit all brought to the point of breaking by
  their suffering,
all whose faith is damaged by their own pain or that of someone else.
We pray for those in hospital or being cared for at home;
for those who manage our health services,
who have to allocate the limited resources they are given.

Be exalted, O God, above the heavens
Let your glory be over all the earth.

Risen, ascended Lord, hear our prayer for all who have died . . .
You judge us with infinite mercy and see us more fully than we know
  ourselves.
May we come to share in your eternal Kingdom.

Be exalted, O God, above the heavens
Let your glory be over all the earth.

Monarch supreme, all authority in heaven and earth owes allegiance to
you. We commend the whole world to your eternal goodness.

PENTECOST (WHIT SUNDAY)

Principal Feast

Pour out your Spirit, O Lord
We will rejoice in you.

Holy Spirit of love and joy,
you came to those gathered at the first Pentecost,
filling them with boldness to speak of your marvellous deeds
in words their hearers could comprehend.
Come to your Church,
that it may proclaim you with conviction
and in lives made holy in your service . . .
Fill us with songs of praise for the wonders of your love.

Pour out your Spirit, O Lord
We will rejoice in you.

Holy Spirit of freedom and peace,
you have inspired men and women through all generations
and provoked them to strive for justice.
Guide the leaders of the nations
and all who exercise power
to work for the benefit of all your people.
Drive from us bitterness and hatred,
that we may live in harmony and concord.

Pour out your Spirit, O Lord
We will rejoice in you.

Holy Spirit of patience, kindness and self-control,
you moved over the waters at creation
and brought forth all that the Word desired.
You empower us to share in your work of bringing to birth the
    Kingdom.
Go between us
and draw together people of every race, language and nation
into a unity of humanity.

Pour out your Spirit, O Lord
We will rejoice in you.

Holy Spirit of healing and wonderful works,
you sustain us with your living power
and renew the face of the earth.
Bring wholeness to all weighed down by oppressions of the mind, body
   or spirit . . .
O Comforter, strengthen all for whom we pray.

Pour out your Spirit, O Lord
We will rejoice in you.

Holy Spirit of faithfulness and truth,
it is through you that we affirm our hope in Jesus risen from the dead.
In this faith we pray for all who have died . . .
Bring us at the last to the place prepared for us in Christ our Lord.

Pour out your Spirit, O Lord
We will rejoice in you.

Holy Spirit of wisdom and generosity, in your power we commit these
prayers through Christ to the gentle mercy of the Father.

TRINITY SUNDAY

Principal Feast

Worship the Lord in the beauty of holiness
May the whole world exalt your name.

God of Glory, Eternal Word and Spirit of Truth,
we stand before your presence made worthy in your grace.
You created the universe and set the world on its course.
In time, you brought all living plants and creatures into being,
moulded planets and galaxies about which we can only dream,
and we delight in all you have made.
Before your might and power we bow in awe and wonder.

Worship the Lord in the beauty of holiness
May the whole world exalt your name.

Creator, Redeemer and Sustainer,
your love overflows to touch even the hairs on our head,
and a leaf does not fall without you noticing.
You call all people to follow the Way of your Son,
and send your Spirit to equip us in the tasks of this ministry.
We pray for the Church,
for *N* our bishop and all set on fire by the good news you bring . . .
Strengthen for service, Lord, all who seek your Kingdom.

Worship the Lord in the beauty of holiness
May the whole world exalt your name.

Holy, Holy, Holy Lord,
God of the powerful and the weak,
we pray for all who take up the mantle of leadership and government.
Give them vision for the broader picture
in which we live, move and have our being.
We pray for justice in law and trading,
for an equal sharing of all the earth affords.
Teach us to model our communal living

100

on the mutual love and regard we see in and between your Triune
Being.

Worship the Lord in the beauty of holiness
May the whole world exalt your name.

God our Father, Son and Holy Spirit,
in the mystery of your Trinity we find our hope in adversity and
    anxiety.
There is no distance too far from you,
no concern too small to you,
no place within us that you cannot reach.
Pour your healing and restoring love
on all who are sick or passing through a time of trial . . .
As the heavens are full of your glory,
so may we find voice to sing your praise.

Worship the Lord in the beauty of holiness
May the whole world exalt your name.

Lord of all time and eternity,
of this moment and what is to come,
we pray for all who have died . . .
Draw us deeper into the wonder of your life
and when you bring your creation to fulfilment in your Son,
grant us a place in that eternity with you.

Worship the Lord in the beauty of holiness
May the whole world exalt your name.

Praise to the Father, who was and is and is to come.
Praise to the Son, in whose embrace we are brought
    to your eternal heart.
Praise to the Spirit, who fills us with the potency of your recreating
    presence.
All glory and honour be to you now and for ever.

CORPUS CHRISTI
THANKSGIVING FOR HOLY COMMUNION

Festival

Thursday after Trinity Sunday

Jesus, our living bread
May we taste and see your goodness.

God of our pilgrimage,
you feed us with the bread of life.
Fill our hearts with the fruit of your abundant goodness
and sanctify our lives, that they may resonate with you.

Jesus, our living bread
May we taste and see your goodness.

God of our mystery,
we pray for the Church;
for *N* our bishop and all ministers of the sacraments . . .
We pray for all who preside at the Eucharist;
those who administer the bread and wine;
those who take Communion to the housebound and those in residential
    homes.
As the Church celebrates and participates in these mysteries of your love,
so may our lives be filled with your glory.

Jesus, our living bread
May we taste and see your goodness.

God of the harvest,
we pray for civic leaders;
for a just and equal sharing of the earth's resources.
We pray for all who work in agriculture and the food industry;
for local shops and those who distribute the fruits of your creation
    around the world.

Jesus, our living bread
May we taste and see your goodness.

God of hospitality,
we pray for all who are hungry – physically and spiritually.
We pray for day centres for the homeless, for lunch clubs for the elderly,
and for our own sharing in fellowship when bread is broken and wine
   outpoured.
Thank you for all who feed our minds and inspire our spirits;
for preachers and those who mediate our feeding on your Word.

Jesus, our living bread
May we taste and see your goodness.

God of our loving,
in the bread, we offer our lives, our bodies and our brokenness;
in the wine, as your blood is poured out for us on the cross,
we offer our pains and the suffering of your world . . .
Heal us and free us to rejoice in the joy of your salvation.

Jesus, our living bread
May we taste and see your goodness.

God of our hope and consolation,
as we commemorate your death until you come again,
we commend to your goodness all who have died . . .
Send your consoling Spirit on those who bear the pains of grief.
May we and all your people be united in this foretaste of your celestial
   banquet
prepared for all in your Kingdom.

Jesus, our living bread
May we taste and see your goodness.

As we rejoice in this celebration of your passion and resurrection, we
offer this sacrifice of prayer to your redeeming love.

CHRIST THE KING

Principal Feast

Sunday before Advent

Lord, your Kingdom come
Your will be done.

Christ in majesty,
all things are fulfilled in you.
We bow before your throne of grace.
Increase our confidence in your redeeming love.
May you rule in our hearts,
as we dedicate all that we are and all that we have in your service.

Lord, your Kingdom come
Your will be done.

Gracious Father,
we pray for the Church, that it may bear convincing witness to its trust
   in you;
that all things find their completion in your Son.
We pray for N our bishop and all who profess faith in your Son . . .
Strengthen us in the power of your Holy Spirit to proclaim your glory,
even in the face of ridicule and persecution.

Lord, your Kingdom come
Your will be done.

Eternal Ruler,
the source and goal of all authority,
we pray for those who exercise power and rule for a time on earth.
We pray for those whose self-understanding is corrupted by the power
   they hold.
May all who govern always be mindful of the responsibility committed
   to their charge,
that they may work for a just and cohesive society.

Lord, your Kingdom come
Your will be done.

Suffering Servant,
you showed your glory in human frailty and suffering.
We pray for all who are enduring a crisis of trust in your providence;
for those who are ground down by ailments of mind, body or spirit . . .
Bless all who seek to be rescued from the power of darkness.

Lord, your Kingdom come
Your will be done.

Lord, from the cross your Son announced, 'It is finished.'
We pray for those who have died and entered the fulfilment of all things
    in your Son . . .
Complete in all your children that which you have begun to work in
    them.

Lord, your Kingdom come
Your will be done.

Rejoicing in Christ in majesty, exalted and reigning in glory, we entrust
all people to your gracious mercy.

Part Two

GENERAL LESSER FESTIVALS, COMMEMORATIONS AND OTHER OCCASIONS

3

Lesser Festivals and Commemorations

———————◆◆◆———————

GENERAL – HOLY MEN AND WOMEN

Holy God
Sanctify us in your love.

God, the source of all holiness,
we praise you for the men and women in whom your light has shone
    throughout the ages.
We thank you for N, for making your presence known in the frailty of
    human life,
sanctified by your redeeming love.
Fill us with your Spirit,
that our hearts may resound with your heavenly glory,
and we may live the life you give.

Holy God
Sanctify us in your love.

Inspire your Church, Lord, with awe and wonder for your holy
    name.
We pray for N our bishop . . .
We give thanks for those whose holiness of life
    makes us feel we have come close to touching the divine,
whose dedication to prayer renews within us a model of holy living.
Teach us to be still in your company,
to know and trust that you are always with us.

Holy God
Sanctify us in your love.

God of truth and justice,
   we pray for those who govern and rule nations,
for community leaders and those with regional responsibility.
Give them courage to face up to necessary decisions,
even when they are unpopular,
wisdom to steer a course when vision is incomplete,
compassion never to overlook those affected by the consequences.

Holy God
Sanctify us in your love.

God of compassion and mercy,
we hold in your presence all for whom our prayers have been asked . . .
We pray for the housebound,
for all whose former stature is unseen and known only to you.
We pray for those whose patience is strained by frustrations
and the pressures that wear down charity.

Holy God
Sanctify us in your love.

Lord of life and hope, we bring before you those who have died . . .
We recall with thanksgiving those whose lives have shone as beacons to
   your glory.
We look forward to the day when we come to share with them
in the eternal banquet of your Kingdom.

Holy God
Sanctify us in your love.

Creator, redeemer and sustaining presence,
eternal three
and Holy God,
as we rejoice with *N* and all the saints,
so we praise you for your goodness.

BISHOPS

Faithful God
Give ear to our prayer.

Christ our true Shepherd,
we give you thanks for N and all who have shepherded your pilgrim
   people;
for those who have led your Church in faithfulness and trust,
who have nurtured your people in the good news of your Son.
Inspire all who encourage the Church in its mission and ministry today.
Refresh us all with zeal for your gospel.

Faithful God
Give ear to our prayer.

Bless those who exercise oversight and supervise the ministry of others.
Give them vision and imagination in shaping the structures of the
   Church
to equip it for its calling.
We pray for N Archbishop of Canterbury, N our bishop,
and all who focus the unity of the Church . . .
Pour out your Spirit on our own church community.
Sustain in your service all who exercise leadership,
all who administer the sacraments,
all who teach, preach and give pastoral care.

Faithful God
Give ear to our prayer.

Everlasting God, we pray for world leaders, our own government and
   councils,
and all whom we elect to political service.
Encourage those who strive for peace and reconciliation;
all who courageously speak the prophetic words of justice.
May the common good be honoured and liberty and equality upheld.

Faithful God
Give ear to our prayer.

We hold in prayer all who are ill in any way,
or for whom our prayers have been particularly asked . . .
Uphold the housebound, the lonely, any searching for direction;
the homeless and routeless.
Be with any losing heart under pressure or who are anxious for the
    future.
Shine in our hearts the light of your saving love.

Faithful God
Give ear to our prayer.

In Christ we remember with thanksgiving all who have died . . .
May your light shine on them for ever,
that those who rest in peace may rise in glory.

Faithful God
Give ear to our prayer.

Celebrating our fellowship with *N* and the great cloud of witnesses that
surround us, we commit all for whom we pray to your loving care.

CHRISTIAN RULERS

Sovereign Lord
Let the earth rejoice in your goodness.

In the cross of Christ we glory and in that alone.
Give grace to your Church to walk in the way of the cross
and to find it none other than the way of life and peace.
We pray for N our bishop, for all who lead us in vision . . .
We pray for spiritual guides, all who nurture faith
and whose counsel enlivens our Christian living.
Hear our song of praise
for all who help ease communication of the gospel in unfamiliar territory
and make good use of the power of access.

Sovereign Lord
Let the earth rejoice in your goodness.

As we commemorate N we pray for all Christian rulers and politicians,
those who bear the weight of authority
and view the office they hold through the eyes of vocation.
We pray for Elizabeth our Queen and all who serve in parliament;
for civil servants and those who assist in the work of government;
for the police and security services, and all who seek to defend our
    freedoms.
Sustain with your protective presence those who combat organized crime
    and all that would oppress us.
We pray for the courts that administer justice;
for judges and magistrates,
those who defend the accused and those who set out the case against
    them;
for those awaiting trial or to bring a case of dispute.
We pray for impartial and fair judgements.

Sovereign Lord
Let the earth rejoice in your goodness.

We bring before you our homes and neighbourhoods;
the communities to which we belong.

May we seek to fashion our lives on Christ and his Kingdom.
We pray for grace in the struggles and conflicts of life,
that we may stand firm for truth and be gracious in our approach to our
    neighbours.
We pray for all community groups,
those who strengthen the fabric of our common life;
all who are easily overlooked or ignored;
all at the margins of society.

Sovereign Lord
Let the earth rejoice in your goodness.

Look with mercy on those damaged by battles and conflicts;
all who continue to bear the scars of warfare or hostilities of any kind.
Preserve those attacked by illness or any kind of adversity . . .
Hold before us the cross of Christ,
that it may be a comfort and support in our weakness.

Sovereign Lord
Let the earth rejoice in your goodness.

Lord, you have already won for us the victory.
We lay before you those who have died . . .
Lift all who have been overcome by violence,
all who have died for the protection of others.
Raise us all in your love.

Sovereign Lord
Let the earth rejoice in your goodness.

King of kings and Lord of lords, as we commemorate N and all your
saints, so we entrust all your people to your saving love.

HOLINESS REVEALED IN MARRIAGE
AND FAMILY LIFE

We trust in you, O Lord
We rejoice in your name.

God our Father and Mother,
you draw us nearer to you as a mother gathers her children.
May your Church display a good model for family life in its love and
   care,
its nurture and support of all who come to it.
We pray for those being prepared for baptism and confirmation,
for godparents and sponsors,
all who nurture faith and set an example of godly living.
We pray for *N* our bishop and all who lead our churches . . .

We trust in you, O Lord
We rejoice in your name.

We pray for governments, for those whose policies affect family life.
We pray that all will honour and respect marriage vows.
We pray for working hours and practices that allow time for children
   and home,
for living and loving.
We pray for schemes which aim to develop parents in their care,
and support those having difficulty coping with challenging children
or with the responsibilities of being parents . . .
We pray for schools and give thanks for the support they give to parents
   and children.

We trust in you, O Lord
We rejoice in your name.

Bless our homes and families, that they may be places of love, security
   and peace.
We pray for all whose home life is troubled or disturbed;
for those in broken homes and those tempted to stray.
We pray for children in care homes, and for foster families;

for social workers, health visitors and midwives;
for all who support new parents.
May we draw our example and strength from your great love for us.

We trust in you, O Lord
We rejoice in your name.

We pray for all who are ill at this time or in any other kind of need;
for all whose stress is taken out on those closest to them.
We pray for children's hospitals and hospices.
Send your blessing on all for whom we pray . . .

We trust in you, O Lord
We rejoice in your name.

We commend to your goodness all who have died;
those we have known and those who have no one to pray for them . . .
Complete in them that which you have begun
and draw us all to share in your eternal Kingdom.

We trust in you, O Lord
We rejoice in your name.

In union with *N* and all your saints throughout the ages, we commit our
prayers to you.

MARTYRS

Lord of life and love
Into your hands we commend our spirits.

Gracious God,
we thank you for N and all who over the centuries have followed the
    way of the cross
through being faithful to the gospel in the face of martyrdom.
We pray for Christians who face persecution today;
for all who are unable to practise their faith freely.
Keep your Church mindful of where its true treasure lies.
We pray for N our bishop . . .
Inspire us to joyful praise and a lively hope in Jesus Christ.
Release in all your people the image of your glory.

Lord of life and love
Into your hands we commend our spirits.

Give courage to all who struggle against corruption and vice.
We pray for those who have responsibility of government.
We pray for those tempted to misuse their power,
to persecute those who stand in their way;
for all drawn to violence and the abuse of another's dignity
    and human rights.
We pray for journalists and all who contribute responsibly
    to the free press,
sometimes at personal risk and cost;
for those who keep us informed about events and developments in this
    country and abroad.
Sustain with your Spirit all who stand for justice
and uphold law and order without partiality.

Lord of life and love
Into your hands we commend our spirits.

We pray for all who take an interest in their neighbourhoods and
    communities;

for residents' associations, local councils and local societies.
We give thanks for all that strengthens the bonds that unite us
and for all that helps to improve our environment.
Keep us hospitable and open to those whose aspirations
   differ from our own.
We pray for friends and loved ones near and far.

Lord of life and love
Into your hands we commend our spirits.

Be with all who walk through the valley of the shadow of death,
all who suffer at the hands of others and have entered the darkness of
   inhumanity.
We pray for victims of abuse, those deemed expendable,
and those whose hearts are hard and unmoved by cries for mercy;
for any who have committed murder or are drawn to violence.

Lord of life and love
Into your hands we commend our spirits.

We lay before you all whom we carry in our heart's concern . . .
Grant them the joy of your saving love and restore in them the fullness
   of life.
We pray for those who continue to carry the scars of hostility;
for all imprisoned by fears, by addictions, by infirmity or bars of the
   mind.
Free us from the chains that bind us to live for your glory.

Lord of life and love
Into your hands we commend our spirits.

We remember with thankful hearts all who have died . . .
We give thanks for all who have given their lives courageously and with
   self-sacrifice
in the service of others and with faithfulness to your gospel.
We pray for any who have died through war and violence.
Draw all your children to the eternal banquet of your heavenly
   Kingdom.

Lord of life and love
Into your hands we commend our spirits.

God of justice and charity, as we rejoice with *N* and all your saints and martyrs down the centuries, we lay our prayers before your throne of grace.

MEN AND WOMEN OF LEARNING

God of wisdom and understanding
Our delight is in your Word.

God of truth and justice,
give us the eyes of faith, that we may see more fully the wonders of
your love.
We thank you for N and all who enrich the Church through their
devout scholarship.
We pray for places of prayer and learning;
for those who expand our horizons and help us see in greater depth.
Teach us to delight in knowledge of your truth and to be open to its
challenge.

God of wisdom and understanding
Our delight is in your Word.

We pray for the Church;
for space for reflection and to see differently in the light of your gospel.
We pray for N our bishop and all with whom we share the name of
Christ . . .
Give your Church courage to speak out where it is needed.

God of wisdom and understanding
Our delight is in your Word.

Lord, your Kingdom is established in the heavens.
We pray for all to whom we give the responsibility of government,
locally and nationally,
and all who represent us internationally.
We pray for our communities,
for all that helps to build a cohesive society,
giving thanks for those who provide stability and continuity through
long-established roots,
and those who bring fresh eyes from further afield.
We pray for places of education and learning;
for teachers and mentors, all who influence the young;
for places of adult education and those retraining for new jobs.

120

God of wisdom and understanding
Our delight is in your Word.

Lord, your Son endured the anguish of the cross.
Hear our prayer for all who find their own cross hard to bear;
all who are alone and far from home;
those whose faith has grown dull.
Pour your healing presence on all who cry to you . . .

God of wisdom and understanding
Our delight is in your Word.

Heavenly Father, as our hearts long for you,
we give thanks for all who rejoice in your eternal presence.
Among the departed . . .
Grant that we may come to share in your eternal Kingdom.

God of wisdom and understanding
Our delight is in your Word.

Celebrating your love made known in *N* and all your saints, we entrust
ourselves and all people to your transforming love.

MISSIONARIES

God our righteousness and strength
We sing your praise among all people.

Generous God, you go before us and prepare the way.
There is no place where you are not already there.
We give thanks for our inheritance with the saints in glory;
for the gospel of Jesus Christ
and all who have toiled in love to kindle its flame in this land and
throughout the world.
We give thanks for the spiritual traditions and insights
which have grown and been nurtured in this land . . .
We pray for all who are drawn to tread the pilgrim's path to the holy
sites.
May the faith that burnt brightly in the heart of N set us ablaze today.

God our righteousness and strength
We sing your praise among all people.

We pray for the Church,
for N our bishop and all who inspire us in our faith;
for theologians and those involved in training for ministry and mission;
for all seeking ways to communicate your gospel anew in word and
deed,
to share the great treasure we have in your Son.
May your Church speak of your generous bounty and goodness . . .
Raise up holy and loving missionaries today,
that your glory may be proclaimed afresh in this land.

God our righteousness and strength
We sing your praise among all people.

We pray for political leaders, monarchs,
and those who have the responsibility of government;
for their advisers and counsellors.
Help them to listen, to be still and wonder at your awesome presence
among us.
May peace with justice reign.

God our righteousness and strength
We sing your praise among all people.

We hold in prayer all who are frail;
any troubled in mind, body or spirit.
We pray for all overwhelmed by oppressive relationships, by addictions
and poverty,
all whose experience of faith has damaged them or turned them cold.
By name, we pray for . . .
Pour upon us your healing and life-giving Spirit.

God our righteousness and strength
We sing your praise among all people.

Renew in our hearts songs of thanks and praise.
We pray for those nearing the hour of their death;
for any who are frightened or in severe pain.
We pray for those who have died;
any whose memory is always with us . . .
Grant to the departed the brightness of your new day,
and to all who mourn the comfort of your light made manifest in the
saints in glory.

God our righteousness and strength
We sing your praise among all people.

Righteous God, as we rejoice with *N* and all the saints and missionaries
of this land, we entrust our prayers to your redeeming love.

PASTORS

Loving Lord
Hear the prayers we bring.

Christ our friend and brother,
you came among us as one who serves,
and call your followers to imitate your way of love and truth.
We give you thanks for N and all who share in the ministry of pastoral
  care today;
all who devote themselves to your service and the service of others;
those whose dedication inspires others.
We pray for all who labour with faith and dedication away from the
  limelight;
for those who serve faithfully among the poor, the easily forgotten
  and ignored.

Loving Lord
Hear the prayers we bring.

Hear our prayer for those who exercise a ministry of oversight in the
  Church,
for N our bishop, for all clergy and those with whom they minister . . .
We give thanks for those who expand our understanding of
  psychological and spiritual dynamics at work in us all and so resource
  pastoral ministry;
for advisers in pastoral care and deliverance.
We pray for those who are there
when we need to unburden distresses that have been shared.

Loving Lord
Hear the prayers we bring.

God of wisdom, inspire with your justice those chosen to fill positions of
  government;
those with responsibility for health care provision and community
  services.
We pray for hospital and hospice chaplains;

those who administer welfare and social support;
any who are abused by those who come to them in need.
We pray for day care facilities and night shelters;
for those who work with the marginalized and most difficult to care for
or whose behaviour is challenging.

Loving Lord
Hear the prayers we bring.

God of compassion, we hold in your presence all facing increasing
    infirmity,
who can no longer do what they once could.
We pray for those having to rely on others where they were self-
    sufficient before;
for the housebound and those who receive Communion at home;
for all who are lonely or depressed, the suicidal and those who have lost
    hope . . .
Strengthen your children in their frailty and bring the joy of your saving
    love.

Loving Lord
Hear the prayers we bring.

Risen Lord, we pray for all your faithful servants who have died
and now share in your eternal banquet.
We pray for loved ones departed . . .
Console all who are deeply troubled by grief.
May Christ the morning star give comfort and peace
    at the hour of our death.

Loving Lord
Hear the prayers we bring.

Rejoicing in company with *N* and all the saints, we place all for whom
we pray into your loving arms of mercy.

RELIGIOUS

Lord of hope and fount of wisdom
Incline your ear to our prayer.

Heavenly Father,
your Son called his disciples friends.
Draw us ever deeper into the love that shares of its very self,
the love that helps us be ourselves more fully and grow in grace.
We give thanks for those whose love has opened our eyes to your
    eternal glory among us,
for N and all who dedicate themselves to contemplative prayer
    and the religious life.
May their example inspire the Church to be still and trust in you alone.
Give us patience and confidence to stand at the door of hope in stilled
    silence,
and shine into our hearts the light of your love in Jesus Christ.

Lord of hope and fount of wisdom
Incline your ear to our prayer.

We give thanks for the hospitality that shares of its wealth and poverty,
that welcomes and embraces strangers as unknown friends,
as angels and Christ himself.
We pray for those who seek to extend hands across all barriers that
    divide;
for all who prepare the way for peace.
We pray for politicians, rulers and community leaders.
Help us to realize our dependency on you,
to do what is required to promote your Kingdom.
We give thanks for all who help us set our sights higher
    than might otherwise be the case.
Give us the courage we need to follow your call,
whatever obstacles or hostility it may trigger.

Lord of hope and fount of wisdom
Incline your ear to our prayer.

126

We pray for religious houses and places of spiritual renewal,
for all who mother and father us in our faith,
for N our bishop and those who lead our communities of faith . . .
Help us to make space in our daily lives
where we may delight in your goodness and glory.
We pray for places set aside as holy ground,
for this church, this house of prayer.
May we never take it nor the vibrancy of its life for granted.

Lord of hope and fount of wisdom
Incline your ear to our prayer.

God of compassion and mercy,
create in us space for all who are ill or in special need.
We pray for all with disabilities or who are differently abled,
who open our eyes to truths we would otherwise miss . . .
We give thanks and pray for all carers,
all who watch and wait by the side of someone close,
or ensure that they are not alone.
Strengthen your children in their frailty and bring the joy
   of your saving love.

Lord of hope and fount of wisdom
Incline your ear to our prayer.

In our heavenly Father's house there are many rooms.
We pray for those who now share in its shelter . . .
May we with them come to abide with you in glory.

Lord of hope and fount of wisdom
Incline your ear to our prayer.

In union with N and holy men and women of every age, we offer our
prayers to your gracious mercy.

SOCIAL REFORMERS

God of justice
Hear the cry of your people.

God of our salvation,
your justice flows like rivers and your righteousness as an ever-flowing
   stream.
We give you thanks for *N* and for men and women down the ages
whose faith has inspired them to challenge and change unjust structures
   of the world.
Raise up, we pray, men and women with courage to speak prophetic
   words today.
We pray for *N* our bishop
and all who speak to the Church and for the Church on social issues;
for projects and groups transforming the social landscape
in areas of great need . . .
May the good news we proclaim announce release and freedom for all.

God of justice
Hear the cry of your people.

Righteous Lord, guide all who seek to live their Christian calling
   through political service – locally, nationally and internationally.
Strengthen the bonds that unite us into a common humanity.
Forgive us the sins and legacy of past abuses
and lead us into the ways of your peace.

God of justice
Hear the cry of your people.

Liberating God, you set your people free from slavery in Egypt
and drew them into the land of promise.
Be with all who cry for freedom;
those enslaved by oppressive trade practices or working conditions;
those whose dignity and worth is sold or exploited;
those who lack adequate housing or with poor access to services
   they need.

Proclaim your release to any locked in by prejudice or fear.
Give us courage to strive for reform and respect for all.

God of justice
Hear the cry of your people.

Lord, whose compassion never fails,
Pour out your healing presence on all weighed down by illness or
    infirmity.
As your Son showed favour to the woman who anointed his body
    with oil,
so may those who minister to the needs of others
    be blessed in their labours of loving service.
Hear our prayer for all who cry out in pain or distress . . .
As you bless us, so may we hear your words of healing and release.

God of justice
Hear the cry of your people.

Loving God, we commend to your goodness all who have died . . .
We pray for all who are terminally ill and those who keep vigil
    by their side;
for any frightened of dying.
May Christ the morning star give comfort and peace
    at the hour of our death.

God of justice
Hear the cry of your people.

As we exalt and magnify your holy name, with *N* and the whole
household of God, we place all people before your abiding love.

SPIRITUAL WRITERS AND MYSTICS

Lord of glory
With heart and voice we praise you.

God of mystery and love,
with wonder at your mighty presence
we come to raise a faithful anthem of prayer and praise.
Give to your Church due reverence for your holy name.
We give thanks for N and all who lift our senses to awe and wonder.
We praise you for men and women who through the ages have been so
    absorbed in you
that their writings have inspired and enlivened your Church.
May your Spirit continue to inspire men and women today
    to offer words through which your Church can sing your praises.
So fill our hearts with passion for your gospel,
that the fire of your love may be kindled and set ablaze within us.

Lord of glory
With heart and voice we praise you.

O Lord God of hosts, the heavens resound with your praise.
Give to your Church the gift of discernment
to recognize spiritual insights and distinguish them from delusions.
We pray for N our bishop and all spiritual leaders;
for places of pilgrimage,
where you are encountered in fresh ways and ways that refresh your
    people . . .
Bless all who help us to be aware of our communion with Christ
and lead us to grow in our journey of faith:
teachers and mentors, spiritual guides and all who help us to pray.

Lord of glory
With heart and voice we praise you.

Gracious God, your love sets us ablaze and ignites a fire within that
    inspires us to action.
Send your transforming Spirit on our politicians and community leaders.

Help us to see and value the inner qualities, beyond image and headlines.
We pray for all whose counsel helps to draw out the visionary and
higher calling.

Lord of glory
With heart and voice we praise you.

Lord, your Son endured such pains on the cross for our redemption.
We hold before you all who are distressed by afflictions of the body,
mind or spirit . . .
We give you thanks for those who find ways to rise above or overcome
limitations,
to allow gifts to flourish.
We pray for those easily written off,
those who do not conform to fashions and designer lifestyles.
Send your healing grace on us all
and in all our vulnerability fill our hearts with songs of thankfulness
and praise.

Lord of glory
With heart and voice we praise you.

We commend to your eternal goodness all who have died . . .
We pray for those who are deeply troubled by grief and those who fear
death.
Bless all who mourn;
give them grace to let go into new life.
Be our guard and keeper at the ending of the day.

Lord of glory
With heart and voice we praise you.

As we glorify your name, in communion with *N* and all the saints, we
offer these our prayers before your throne of grace.

TEACHERS OF THE FAITH

Teach us your way, O Lord
That we may walk in your truth.

God the Father, God the Son, God the Holy Spirit,
Holy and blessed Trinity,
draw us into the mystery of your love.
We give thanks for N and all who inspire our faith
and open our minds to the riches of your gracious presence.
We pray for N our bishop, for all theologians and those who open the
    scriptures for us . . .
Inspire us with your Holy Spirit
as new discoveries and wonders unfold a fuller vision of your glory.

Teach us your way, O Lord
That we may walk in your truth.

Wonderful Counsellor, Prince of Peace,
guide with your wisdom all who carry the burden of leadership;
all who rule and bear the responsibility of government.
We pray for their advisers and those involved with think-tanks;
for all who resource decision-making.
Give vision and discernment
to all who have to steer a course through confusing
    and conflicting voices.

Teach us your way, O Lord
That we may walk in your truth.

Lord of truth and understanding,
we pray for places of education and learning;
for schools and colleges, for further and higher institutions;
for study courses and imaginative programmes for life-long learning.
We pray for all who have difficulties to overcome – prejudices,
    impediments, excessive pressures.
We pray for teachers and assistants in the classroom;
for school governors and those who provide administrative support;

for education authorities and all who determine decisions of policy.
We thank you for teachers who have inspired us and unlocked doors for
  our learning.

Teach us your way, O Lord
That we may walk in your truth.

In your mercy, Lord, be with those suffering from any kind of sickness
  or adversity;
all who are facing terminal illnesses or a decline in their abilities.
We pray for all whose disabilities restrict their contribution
or open insights the more able-bodied miss . . .

Teach us your way, O Lord
That we may walk in your truth.

With thankful hearts we commend to your eternal goodness those who
  have died . . .
Grant us with the faithful departed a place in your heavenly Kingdom.

Teach us your way, O Lord
That we may walk in your truth.

Eternal Wisdom, as we rejoice with *N* and all the saints, we place our
trust in your saving love.

THOSE WORKING WITH THE POOR AND UNDERPRIVILEGED

Righteous God
Set us free to serve you.

Gracious God,
keep your Church mindful of where its true treasure lies.
We pray for all who dedicate themselves in the service of others;
for deacons, pastoral assistants, all who visit and care in the name of
  Christ.
Teach us to love mercy and to walk humbly with you.
We pray for N our bishop . . .
Give to your Church courage and passion to speak for those who have
  no voice
or are frequently ignored.
Inspire men and women to work for the transformation of our society.

Righteous God
Set us free to serve you.

Generous God, we pray for all who shape public policy;
those responsible for housing and ensuring adequate standards and safety.
We pray for all straining to make ends meet on benefits or low pay;
those seeking paid employment;
for trade unions and organizations that represent the rights and interests
  of employees,
especially any whose work is exploited or safety endangered.
Lord, let your justice flow, that your people may rejoice in your
  abundant goodness.

Righteous God
Set us free to serve you.

Lord of all, we pray for our communities;
for all in sheltered accommodation, any unable to cope on their own.
Look in mercy on those who find that old age brings particular
  difficulties;

those with disabilities of mind or body;
any suffering from breakdowns and all who feel at the margins of our
    society;
for carers at home, for young carers and those who offer support.
We pray for all who live in impoverished and deprived surroundings.
May the good news you bring to the poor set us free to proclaim your
    favour.

Righteous God
Set us free to serve you.

Lord, we lay before you all whom we carry in our hearts . . .
We pray for any struggling to cope,
for those who find it difficult to ask for help or to know where to turn.
Grant us the joy of your saving love and restore in us the fullness of life.

Righteous God
Set us free to serve you.

With thankful hearts we remember all who have died . . .
We pray for those who have given their lives courageously and with
    self-sacrifice
in the service of others and with faithfulness to the gospel.
Draw them and all your children to the eternal banquet of your
    heavenly Kingdom.

Righteous God
Set us free to serve you.

As we exalt and magnify your holy name, with N and the whole
household of God, we place our prayers before your enduring love.

4

Other Occasions

—◆—

HARVEST

Generous God
We will trust in your bountiful goodness.

For the gifts of your creation,
fruits in their season,
rains and rivers to water the earth,
sunshine to ripen and warm:
all that sustains life,
we give you thanks and praise.

Generous God
We will trust in your bountiful goodness.

For our stewardship of natural resources,
our farming and industry,
our trading and sharing,
our labours and leisure:

Generous God
We will trust in your bountiful goodness.

For the hungry and homeless,
our caring and sharing of burdens,
for governments and all in positions of power:

Generous God
We will trust in your bountiful goodness.

Lord of the harvest,
send labourers to be ministers of your gospel.
For the Church . . .
for spiritual food,
bread to break
and wine outpoured:

Generous God
We will trust in your bountiful goodness.

For healing of mind and body;
medical practitioners and all who apply their skills to developing
     remedies;
for all in special need . . .

Generous God
We will trust in your bountiful goodness.

With thankful hearts
we commend to you all who have died . . .
Gather them in your eternal harvest in gentleness and peace.

Generous God
We will trust in your bountiful goodness.

Rejoicing in your goodness, we trust in your bountiful care.

MEMORIAL OR BEREAVEMENT

For use at a service when the bereaved are invited to remember the departed.

With thankful hearts we bring our prayers to our heavenly Father.

Lord of life and hope
Reveal your glory.

For all who have given us so much and whom we see no longer;
for the times we have laughed and cried;
for all we have given and all we have received;
for the love that has been shared:
we give you thanks.

Lord of life and hope
Reveal your glory.

For all who bear the pain of parting;
for grief suddenly or untimely borne;
for parents who have lost children;
for the stillborn and pregnancies that did not go full term;
for all who have been struck by tragedy:

Lord of life and hope
Reveal your glory.

For all who feel lost or whose life is shattered by the darkness
    of their grief;
for the despairing, any who have lost their hold on hope;
for all finding it difficult to cope on their own or alone;
for all traumatized by the suffering of another:

Lord of life and hope
Reveal your glory.

For friends who listen,
for bereavement counsellors and all who help us find our way again;

for all who hold us when support is needed;
for all who care for the dying with dignity and love:

Lord of life and hope
Reveal your glory.

For relationships that are fractured,
disputes that seem so silly or so important;
for pains that are too raw to be ignored.
Forgive us the harsh words said which were not wise words,
injuries inflicted and endured.

Lord of life and hope
Reveal your glory.

For a vision to live in the future;
for courage to let go of what belongs to the past,
and for a place to store treasured memories.
Free us from the chains that bind us or hold us back
and help us to live in anticipation of heaven in the joy of your
    Kingdom.

Lord of life and hope
Reveal your glory.

As we celebrate our citizenship of heaven, we commit all our prayers to
your gracious mercy.

Suggested Further Resources

Atwell, R. (compiler), *Celebrating the Saints: Daily Spiritual Readings for the Calendar of the Church of England*, Norwich: Canterbury Press, 1998.

Darch, J. H. and Burns, S. K., *Saints on Earth: A Biographical Companion to Common Worship*, London: Church House Publishing, 2004.

Jones, K., *The Saints of the Anglican Calendar*, Norwich: Canterbury Press, 2000.

Brother Tristram SSF (ed.), *Exciting Holiness: Collects and Readings for the Festivals and Lesser Festivals of the Church of England, the Church of Ireland, the Scottish Episcopal Church and the Church in Wales*, 2nd edn, Norwich: Canterbury Press, 2003. The first edition (1997) is also available at <www.excitingholiness.org>.